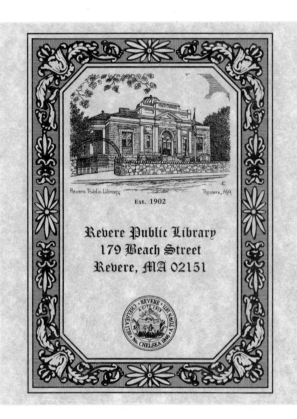

HOLIDAYS

*Days of Significance for
All Americans*

HOLIDAYS

Days of Significance for
All Americans

EDITED BY
Trevor Nevitt Dupuy , ed,

394. 26

Franklin Watts, Inc.
575 Lexington Avenue, New York, N.Y. 10022

CONTENTS

Contents

Contents

PREFACE

MERRILL F. HARTSHORN, EXECUTIVE SECRETARY,

NATIONAL COUNCIL FOR THE SOCIAL STUDIES

TEACHERS have long realized that holidays give an excellent opportunity to present valuable historical material to young children. Holiday observances constitute some of the most rewarding and best-remembered experiences that children have in the elementary school. Dealing as they do with outstanding people and significant events in our history, holidays provide an ideal vehicle for arousing the interest of children and establishing a climate for learning. They can make the past exciting and history come alive so that it is both meaningful and vital.

A cardinal principle in teaching any historical material is that it must be accurate and authentic. Teaching about holidays is no exception to this rule. Teachers should not be guilty of presenting myths, folktales, and legend as history, nor should they present exaggerated or distorted facts in connection with holidays. The truth and facts are exciting enough.

The study of holidays and their observance in school programs can make a most important contribution to a basic objective of education. That is, to acquaint children with their rich cultural heritage and to develop in each individual a deep appreciation of his inheritance of democracy. In these days no goal of education is more important than this objective which puts meaning into our life and establishes endur-

1

ing values which will stand each individual and our country in good stead in a world of conflicting ideologies.

This book renders a valuable service to the busy elementary school teacher who does not have the time or resources to verify the historical scholarship on a wide variety of topics connected with holidays. The authors selected to write this series of essays on holidays are all outstanding historians, each having a special interest in the topic about which he is writing. Further, the editor has selected not only some of the better-known holidays, but has chosen examples of other holidays we should know about if we are to gain an understanding and appreciation of the rich and diverse cultural heritage that has made us a nation of which we can be proud.

This volume is an important contribution to the literature on holidays for elementary school teachers. Here in a single volume the teacher of young children has a resource on which he can rely in developing a program that will inspire children and arouse their interest in learning more about the history of their country.

INTRODUCTION

Holidays has been written primarily for schoolteachers who are searching for ways to transmit—meaningfully, objectively, and without overtones or pressures of propaganda—those values inherent in American history: patriotism, heroism, self-reliance, and tolerance, to name but a few. Knowing the nature of conflicting demands on the time of busy teachers, the Historical Evaluation and Research Organization (HERO) has drawn together brief, pithy essays that are easy to read and from which historical outlines clearly emerge.

One aim has been to make people and events of the past understandable to children of today in terms that are personalized and relevant to the modern environment in which they live. Another aim has been to help teachers explain controversial issues without bias.

Some of the information in *Holidays* will be entirely new to many teachers. We have included, for instance, regularly celebrated American holidays for all races, creeds, and regions across the entire nation. Among these are: Alamo Day, celebrating the memory of valiant Mexican-Texans and Anglo-Americans who died together for the principle of self-government; United Nations Day and Pan-American Day, which symbolize world unity and peace; American Indian Day and Discovery Day, neither widely celebrated, but undeniably American. From these and other stories youngsters can start to learn about their privileges and responsibilities as members of a pluralistic, democratic society. They will also begin to establish a useful basis of historical knowledge upon which they can build in subsequent school years.

We particularly hope that the book will serve elementary

3

school teachers who are endeavoring to implant the first seeds of historical awareness in very young children. We hope, too, that intermediate, junior high, and senior high school teachers and students will find it useful as a flexible basic reference. It can, for instance, be read silently for background; the narrative passages can be read aloud in whole or in part; and specific articles can be consulted for isolated facts. As a single source, or with other teaching materials, *Holidays* should be useful for planning social studies units, enriching assembly programs, and stimulating creative ideas in order to bridge the gap between the events of yesterday and those of today.

In their collaborative effort to make this book short and functional, the authors were faced with painful decisions in choosing what to include and what to emphasize in a very few words. To them I give thanks for their brevity and their cooperation. To the reader I say that *Holidays* was never intended to be an all-inclusive reference book; it was conceived as a source of soundly based ideas which are entertaining and provoking while at the same time practical and convenient to use as a basis for teaching.

In organizing this book, we have been assisted not only by members of HERO's Educational Consultant Team, but also by a number of individual elementary school teachers and school administrators throughout the country. I wish to express our great appreciation for their contributions.

Finally, I wish to express my thanks to Mary F. Hoyt. Not only has she contributed one of the important articles in this book, she has also shared with me the editorial burdens. To her, more than anyone else, is due the credit for developing the concept of this book into a useful, integrated, coherent text.

T. N. Dupuy

ROBERT E. LEE'S BIRTHDAY

(January 19)

CLIFFORD S. DOWDEY

IN MANY STATES, January 19 is celebrated as the birthday of Robert E. Lee, a man who possessed such nobility of character, such magnanimity of spirit, that those against whom he fought honored him as a great American. During the Civil War, he came to symbolize the ideal for which the Southern people were fighting; in the postwar years of dislocation and poverty, he came to symbolize their "lost cause." Even though he went to war reluctantly, he was judged by many to be the greatest military genius of all time; yet his ultimate achievement was as a man of peace.

In the manorhouse at Stratford Hall Plantation, in Westmoreland County, Virginia, the southwest corner chamber was called "the mother's room." This handsomely proportioned room, the walls paneled to the high ceiling, opened into a nursery and formed a small suite. From the time that the huge mansion had been built, in 1725, mothers had borne Lee children in that room, including two signers of the Declaration of Independence. On a bitterly cold January 19, 1807, with wind blowing off the Potomac, Ann Hill Carter Lee, daughter of the richest planter in Virginia, gave birth to a brown-eyed boy, whom she named after her two brothers Robert and Edward. This child, Ann Lee's fifth, was born to the greatest heritage in Virginia and probably on the continent—for in that eighteenth year of the new republic, Vir-

5

ginia was the largest, most powerful state in the nation, and the Lees were among its most illustrious leaders.

But Robert Edward Lee was dispossessed of this heritage by the financial disgrace of his father, and this dislocation became a major influence in his life. He was only two years old when his father went to jail for debts. (Born of the most distinguished family in Virginia, handsome and vital, "a man of splendid talents," Lee's father had won the soubriquet of "Light-Horse Harry" as a cavalry leader during the Revolutionary War, and was three times governor of Virginia.) To run her home and educate her children, Ann Lee, who had been left a trust fund by her wealthy and influential father, was forced to the most stringent economies, and Robert adopted her frugal habits. All of his life, waste was abhorrent to him: waste of time, waste of motion, and waste of self. With his motivation to excel, and his religious convictions, he regarded each task as a duty assigned by God. In his teens, as his mother became an invalid, he was her companion and nurse and, in attending her, displayed the compassion which characterized him throughout life.

When he entered West Point at eighteen, he was soon recognized as a natural leader whom fellow cadets regarded as beyond envy. He was tall and classically handsome; and there was an aura of strength and composure about everything he did. Graduating as the ranking cadet in his class, the second highest in marks, he was the first and only student ever to complete the four years without a demerit.

The mold was set when he entered the Army as a second lieutenant. In the Army he served mostly in the Engineers. During the Mexican War, he was the only junior officer whom Commanding General Winfield Scott asked to serve on his staff and so distinguished himself that Scott said he was "the very best soldier I ever saw in the field."

Early in his Army life he married Mary Anne Randolph Custis, heiress of the Arlington Plantation across the river from Washington and whose father, George Washington Parke Custis, was the grandson of Martha Washington and the adopted son of George Washington. Robert and Mary Lee had seven children, four girls and three boys, and in 1859, on the death of Custis, the beautiful Arlington estates came to Lee's family.

When the long-brewing conflict between the northern and southern sections of the Union came to an open break in early 1861, seven states of the Lower South seceded from the Republic, and the incoming President, Abraham Lincoln, resolved to prevent their secession by armed force. Lee, like the majority of Virginians, was caught in the middle.

Although slavery was an important issue between the North and the South, Lee had no stake in this. He had freed the four slaves that he had personally inherited and in 1861, in executing Mr. Custis' will, he was emancipating the slaves that Custis had owned. Nor did Lee believe in secession.

Lee, like many other Virginians, was distressed and dismayed by the strain of conflicting loyalties which he experienced, following the secession of the seven states to the South. Like a majority of other Southerners, and some Northerners, Virginians did not believe that the founders of their sovereign commonwealth had surrendered the rule of its internal affairs to a central government. Whether or not they agreed with secession, and opinion was almost evenly divided upon this score, they did not believe that the central government had the right to use force to keep the seceding states in the Union.

Virginia remained in the Union until Lincoln called on all loyal states for volunteers to make war against the seceding states. Then, faithful to its concept of the rights of sovereign states, Virginia seceded. A few days earlier, Lee had been unofficially offered the command of an army to be raised for the invasion of the rebellious states. Lee declined the offer and, making the painful decision that loyalty to his state took precedence over his loyalty to the nation, he resigned his commission as colonel of the First United States Cavalry. He then offered his services to Virginia, saying: "I will never again lift my sword save in defense of my native State." He

7

was immediately offered command of Virginia's armed forces.

The Confederacy was five months old when Virginia joined it. As the Confederate army absorbed Virginia's troops, Lee was assigned to a variety of duties "under the direction of the President," Jefferson Davis, and for several months was the President's principal military adviser. It was not until June 1, 1862, when McClellan's army had advanced to within six miles of Richmond, that Lee was put in command of the troops in Virginia. A month later, by his victory in the Seven Days' Battle, he broke the siege of Richmond and forced McClellan's army into retreat. He next defeated the combined Federal forces in Virginia at the Second Battle of Bull Run (Manassas) and cleared the state of invading troops. In doing this he molded a heterogeneous collection of units into the legendary Army of Northern Virginia, one of the finest fighting forces, man for man, in the history of warfare.

In this achievement, Lee brought to the fullest flowering the traits that had always characterized him. His strategy and superb tactics were the product of working at each task until a master plan evolved and then applying himself to the infinite details of its execution. Yet he could make wise, difficult, and complicated decisions in an instant. Beyond his technical brilliance was the quality of leadership: his men held him in a reverence extended to no other officer in the war.

Lee's brilliance affected only part of the war. He commanded the Army of Northern Virginia, only one of several Confederate armies.

His genius lay in maneuver, and this was restricted by the limitations on his authority and by the inability of the Southern people to provide his army with food, clothing, and other necessities. While, from 1862 to the autumn of 1864, he fought off six successive Federal generals, Northern superiority in numbers and armament grew as Lee's army declined. In the bitterly contested 1864 campaign, Grant's

8

army was much larger than Lee's, but in a brilliant defensive campaign Lee fought the Northern general to a standstill. Both sides lost heavily, but Grant could still draw on manpower to lay siege to the Confederates on a thirty-mile front from Richmond to Petersburg. When the siege began, Lee said: "It will be a mere question of time."

The dwindling numbers of his starved, tattered survivors held on until April 2, 1865, when Grant broke their lines, forcing Lee to abandon the two cities and to try a forlorn movement west. The fragments were overrun at Appomattox Court House on Sunday, April 9, and Lee faced the bitterest moment of his life. Magnanimously, Grant made surrender as easy as possible and Lee never appeared in more imposing dignity.

Returning to a devastated land, Lee was faced with the necessity of supporting his wife and three unmarried daughters (one daughter had died during the war). Arlington had been confiscated by the Federal government; the securities that represented his life's savings were almost worthless, and he had no source of income. Turning down lucrative offers of positions that would have used his name, he took over the presidency of Washington College, a small, provincial institution in Lexington, Virginia, bankrupt by the war. There, putting the past behind, he believed he could do the most good for the "future of the South."

At Washington College, in the five years of declining health left him, Lee increased the student body four times over what it had previously been; raised endowments to build the college into a national institution; and introduced technical studies which he believed were needed for building a new South. (The name of the college was changed to Washington and Lee University in 1871.) The true significance of his achievement was its example for the defeated Southern people and the example of his attitude to the whole nation.

In a time of bitterness, when the Southern states were ruled as conquered territories and Virginia became Military

9

District #1 in the Federal Army of Occupation, Lee constantly advocated reconciliation. Although his name was vilified and he was denied citizenship in the new United States, he arose serenely above hostility and urged leaders of both sides to abandon passion and prejudice and return to "the dictates of reason" for the common good. In defeat, he reached the heights of character, and deepened the stream of the American heritage.

FRANKLIN D. ROOSEVELT'S BIRTHDAY — MARCH OF DIMES

(*January 30*)

GUNTHER E. ROTHENBERG

JANUARY 30 is a day of special significance for Americans. It marks the birthday of Franklin Delano Roosevelt, thirty-second President of the United States, and it is also the occasion for the annual March of Dimes, a nationwide drive for funds to combat polio and certain other crippling diseases. During his four terms in office, from 1933 to 1945, President Roosevelt aroused considerable criticism—and the controversy still rages. But there are few who would deny him a major place in American history. The story of how he overcame the dread infantile paralysis to return to politics and reach the highest office in the land constitutes an inspiring account of courage and determination.

The son of a well-to-do family which settled in the Hudson Valley when New York was still a Dutch colony, Roosevelt was born at Hyde Park on January 30, 1882. He attended preparatory school at Groton and in 1904 graduated from Harvard. In 1905, aged twenty-three, he married his twenty-one-year-old fifth cousin once removed, Anna Eleanor Roosevelt. Mrs. Roosevelt was to gain the respect and love of millions all over the world. A woman of great drive, willpower, and social consciousness, she influenced her husband considerably.

11

In 1910, Roosevelt entered politics as a Democrat, and in 1912 he ardently supported Woodrow Wilson's nomination. After Wilson's election, Roosevelt, always interested in things nautical, was appointed Assistant Secretary of the Navy, a post once held by Theodore Roosevelt. In Washington, Franklin D. Roosevelt was much influenced by Wilson's domestic policy of progress and opportunity, the "New Freedom," and by his dreams for international justice and security. In 1920, Roosevelt ran as the Vice-Presidential candidate with Governor James M. Cox of Ohio on the Democratic ticket, but they were defeated by Republicans Warren G. Harding and Calvin Coolidge.

The following year, Roosevelt was stricken by infantile paralysis and for the next six years he waged an uphill fight for recovery. He was greatly helped by taking warm baths at Warm Springs, Georgia, and in 1927 he assisted in establishing the nonprofit Warm Springs Foundation for Infantile Paralysis, incorporated on January 30, 1938. Since then the foundation has conducted its annual March of Dimes drive on this date.

Originally, the aim of the foundation was the prevention of paralytic poliomyelitis and to aid polio sufferers. After twenty years of work, which resulted in the discovery of the Salk and Sabin polio vaccines, the foundation, now called the National Foundation, broadened its field to foster medical research, professional education, and patient care related to certain birth defects, crippling arthritis, and all types of viral diseases.

Throughout his illness, Roosevelt had maintained contact with friends all over the country, laying the foundation for a progressive Democratic Party. In 1928, he successfully ran for governor of New York, was reelected in 1930, and became the Democratic Presidential choice in 1932. After an overwhelming victory over President Herbert Hoover, Roosevelt assumed office on March 4, 1933. By then the Depression, which had begun with the collapse of the stock market in October, 1929, had deepened and the new Chief Executive did not exaggerate when he told the American people in his inaugural address: "Only the foolish optimist can deny the dark realities of the moment." But, asserted the President, vigorous and prompt action would bring improvement and "the only thing we have to fear is fear itself."

Congress was called into special session on March 9, 1933, and by June 16, during the famous "Hundred Days," it passed an unprecedented volume of legislation. Given the urgent needs of the economic situation, most of the measures dealt with immediate relief. After the "Hundred Days," and until World War II diverted his attention, there followed a number of acts implementing Roosevelt's program, which came to be called "the New Deal."

To provide immediate relief, the jobless and hungry were employed on New Deal projects carried on by the Civilian Conservation Corps, the Public Works Administration, and the Works Progress Administration. Farmers were supported by the Agricultural Adjustment Acts (1933, 1938) and the Soil Conservation Act (1936), which paid them to curtail production. A none-too-successful attempt was made to aid industry through the National Industrial Recovery Act (1933), which aimed to reduce domestic competition. Through the Wagner Act (1935), wage-earners gained the right to collective bargaining, while the threat of unemployment and the specter of old age were eased for many by the Social Security Act of 1935. Stock exchanges were controlled and savings protected by the insurance of savings banks. The government moved to regulate public utilities and launched a great experiment combining the generation of power with economic planning through the Tennessee Valley Authority (1933). Controversial when introduced, some of the measures, especially farm support, collective bargaining, and Social Security, became widely accepted and now constitute a basic part of the pattern of American life.

During the 1930's, the mainstay of opposition to the New Deal was the United States Supreme Court, which in 1935 and 1936 struck down a number of administration-sponsored laws. Roosevelt felt that the Court was deliberately obstructive, and after his landslide victory in the election of 1936, in which he carried every state but Maine and Vermont, he asked Congress for power to increase the Court from nine to fifteen judges and to empower him to appoint one additional justice for every judge over seventy. Although the nation had renewed his overall mandate, there was great popular opposition to the "court-packing" proposal and it never was adopted. Even so, the Court soon reversed itself and upheld a vital minimum-wage law. Then too, conservative judges began to retire, allowing the President to make his own appointments.

By this time, however, Roosevelt's main focus was shifting from domestic to international affairs. In Europe, democratic government was faring badly. Since World War I various dictatorships had been established and, encountering little resistance from the Western democracies, Germany and Italy had embarked on a course of naked militaristic aggression. At the same time, Japan, engaged since 1931 in hostilities against China, was becoming more and more ambitious and appeared determined to establish complete control over the Far East. These developments greatly concerned the President; but for the moment there was little he could do. The majority of Americans were committed to isolation and neutrality. Congress passed a series of neutrality acts, and when, in October, 1937, Roosevelt called for a quarantine of the aggressors, he received little popular support.

From the outbreak of war in Europe in September, 1939, military considerations were paramount. The United States favored the democratic cause in Europe but offered little more than moral encouragement to England and France. After the German victories, when England stood alone against a Hitler-dominated Europe, sentiment began to shift and the United States extended military and economic aid, short of war, to Great Britain. In part, this aid was provided by Presidential initiative, but such action now was widely supported by the country which, in November, 1940, reelected Roosevelt to an unprecedented third term. In March, 1941, Roosevelt gained congressional endorsement in the Lend-Lease Act for his plans to make the United States an "arsenal of democracy." Regarding the victory of Hitler and Mussolini as a definite threat to the nation, the government also extended Lend-Lease aid to the Soviet Union when it, too, was attacked by Germany in June, 1941. A more determined stand against Japanese aggression was taken and, in the summer of 1941, President Roosevelt cut off the shipments of vital strategic materials to Japan. The Japanese answered with the attack on Pearl Harbor on December 7, 1941; four days later Germany and Italy declared war on the United States.

The United States was much better prepared for war in 1941 than it had been in 1917. Much credit for this belongs to the President, who, despite bitter opposition in and out of Congress, had pressed for military preparedness. Although badly hurt by the losses sustained during the first weeks of war, the United States recovered rapidly and during the next four years provided the major amount of war materiel, and a great proportion of the military and naval forces, to defeat the enemy.

Roosevelt was an effective war President. As Commander-in-Chief, he appointed an able team of military leaders and carried responsibility for all major political and strategic decisions. He successfully mobilized the country; and during the dark days of 1942 his energy and optimism did much to keep spirits high. He fully realized the enormous potential of American industrial power and, as early as 1940, he endorsed and supported the development of atomic weapons. He ably represented his country in its relations with its allies and participated in a number of top-level wartime conferences with them.

With his reelection to a fourth term in 1944, his concern about the postwar world increased. Recognizing the fearful potential of the new atomic weaponry, he strove to lay the foundations for a lasting peace through the United Nations.

But he died unexpectedly of a massive cerebral hemorrhage before the charter session of the United Nations met in San Francisco.

Whatever his mistakes, his final record was impressive. When Franklin D. Roosevelt assumed office, the United States was going through its darkest hour since the Civil War; when he died the Republic had become the leading world power. This, perhaps, is the best summary of the man.

NATIONAL FREEDOM DAY

(February 1)

CHARLES H. WESLEY

THE WATCH-NIGHT services on New Year's Eve, December 31, 1862, were thronged with Negro church members, waiting for the news of emancipation to be proclaimed, as President Lincoln's Preliminary Proclamation of September 22 had declared. Assemblies were held in anticipation of "The Great Jubilee."

In Washington, D.C., the pastor of Union Bethel Baptist Church told his congregation that he wanted "no one to pray standing . . . but to get down on both knees to thank Almighty God for his freedom and President Lincoln, too."

Booker T. Washington, in his autobiography *Up From Slavery*, describes hearing a United States officer read the Emancipation Proclamation to a group of Negroes. The officer then told them that they were free. Washington's mother, in tears of joy, leaned over and kissed her children. Washington remembered "great rejoicing and thanksgiving and wild scenes of ecstasy. But there was no feeling of bitterness. In fact, there was pity among the slaves for our former masters."

Commanders of colored troops, north and south, read the Emancipation Proclamation to them. One of these announcements was made by General Rufus Saxton to the troops in South Carolina. He said: "It is your duty to carry this good news to your brethren who are still in slavery. Let all your voices like merry bells join loud and clear in the grand chorus

17

of liberty—We are free! We are free!—Until listening, you shall hear the echoes coming back from every cabin in the land—We are free! We are free!"

The Emancipation Proclamation was interpreted by Negroes as the goal of their aspirations, for through it the day of freedom had arrived. They did not study the words of the Proclamation. They were more interested in its intent and purpose. Even Frederick Douglass, the noted Negro abolitionist, did not stress the words of the Proclamation, for he saw "in its spirit a life and power beyond its words." Lincoln himself said later, according to Frank B. Carpenter, his portrait painter, that the Proclamation was "the central act of my Administration and the greatest event of the nineteenth century."

Millions of Negroes had hoped for freedom and this hope became their ideal. They had dared to sing:

> *O Freedom, O Freedom, O Freedom over me,*
> *Before I'll be a slave*
> *I'll be buried in my grave,*
> *And go home to my Father and be free.*

Freedom was their song, their hope, their prayer, and ambition. When it came they rejoiced.

The Emancipation Proclamation was actually a statement of policy, however, not a statement of law, and it did not apply to the nation as a whole. It freed only the slaves in the rebellious Southern states. A change in the Constitution was needed to abolish slavery everywhere.

Action was started in Congress in late 1863. In February, 1864, Senator Lyman Trumbull of Illinois introduced a constitutional amendment based on a section of the Northwest Ordinance of 1787: "There shall be neither slavery nor involuntary servitude in the said territory . . ." Both the Ordinance and the Declaration of Independence were used by the abolitionists in arguing for freedom. The proposal for a constitutional amendment was passed by the Senate by a

18

vote of 38 to 6, but it did not receive the necessary two-thirds vote in the House of Representatives.

On December 8, 1864, President Lincoln asked Congress to reconsider and pass the resolution for a constitutional amendment abolishing slavery. He was supported by the National Union Convention (the wartime name for the Republican Party), which had nominated him as President for a second term; it had put a pledge to abolish slavery in its platform.

In the meantime, the movement continued to grow as three states—Maryland, Missouri, and Louisiana—abolished slavery. Representative James M. Ashley of Ohio, who on December 4, 1863, had introduced an amendment in the House of Representatives abolishing slavery, called up the resolution on January 6, 1865, for consideration in the House of Representatives. The resolution was approved by the House on January 31 after a long debate, and was also approved by the Senate.

When the announcement of the vote was made in the House of Representatives, the Speaker could not preserve order. The *Congressional Globe* described the scene: "The announcement was received by the House and by the spectators with an outburst of enthusiasm. The members of the Republican side of the House instantly sprung to their feet and, regardless of parliamentary rules, applauded with cheers and clapping of hands. The example was followed by the male spectators in the galleries, which were crowded to excess, who waved their hats and cheered loud and long while the ladies by hundreds waved their handkerchiefs."

The House of Representatives adjourned, "in honor of the immortal and sublime event." Antislavery leader Carl Schurz, one of the observers in the galleries, said that this scene was "worthy of the grand event," while Theodore Tilton and Henry Ward Beecher, editors of the *Independent*, declared on February 2, 1865, "We thank God fervently that we have lived to witness this great deed which, when confirmed by the people, will rank as the grandest event of the century."

19

Negroes all over the country were enthusiastic in their approval of the congressional action. Meetings were held, resolutions were adopted, prayers were offered. One of the songs characteristic of this year 1865 was known as *The Freedman's Song:*

> *The Lord He make us free indeed*
> *In His own time an' way;*
> *We plant the rice and cotton seed,*
> *And see it sprout some day;*
> *We know it come, but not the why—*
> *The Lord know more than we;*
> *We 'spected freedom by and by,*
> *And now we all are free.*
> > *Praise the Lord! Praise the Lord!*
> > *For now we all are free!*

The resolution for the proposed amendment was submitted to President Lincoln and was signed by him on February 1, 1865. It was not necessary that the President sign such a resolution, but Lincoln's signature gave added weight to the amendment and showed his concern that it be approved by the states. Secretary of State William H. Seward made the official announcement that the necessary number of states had given their approval on December 18, 1865.

Emancipation Day, January 1, continued to be celebrated annually without any official proclamation. Other days were also celebrated as Freedom Days—January 1, February 1, December 18, August 8, or some other date of local meaning was chosen. The coming of the Union armies into a particular state or the ratification of the Thirteenth Amendment by the state legislature influenced the day celebrated. In Texas, June 19 was a day for festivity and merrymaking by Negroes, especially in sections of the Brazos Valley. The celebration of that day, which was familiarly known as "June Teenth," continued into the 1930's, and in some areas, the 1940's and the 1950's.

The ending of slavery by constitutional amendment was not observed on an official national day until 1948. The moving spirit behind this official action was Major R. R. Wright, Sr., of Philadelphia, Pennsylvania. An educator and bank president, Major Wright was born in Dalton, Georgia, May 16, 1855. He was educated in freedom schools conducted by white missionaries from the North, and at Atlanta University, from which he received the degrees of Bachelor of Arts and Master of Arts. He served as a high school principal and was the first Negro principal of a public high school in Georgia. He was a college president, a bank president, an officer in the Spanish-American War, and the civic leader in the first Freedom Day celebrations in Philadelphia, in 1921.

Major Wright had been a ten-year-old slave boy when slavery was legally abolished. A story is told of his experience in the days following the Civil War in one of the schools run by the Freedman's Bureau. General O. O. Howard, head of the bureau, visited the school in which young Wright was a pupil. When General Howard asked the children what message they would like to send to the people who were contributors to the school, Wright stood and replied, "Tell them we're rising." Wright's life and career fulfilled this message.

Major Wright's efforts to have an official National Freedom Day did not succeed in his lifetime, but in 1948 the congressional resolution for this observance was passed, and President Harry S. Truman designated February 1, the anniversary of Lincoln's signing the resolution for the Thirteenth Amendment, as National Freedom Day. He declared in his proclamation that the Thirteenth Amendment was "a cornerstone in the foundation of our American traditions, and the signing of the resolution is a landmark in the nation's effort to fulfill the principles of freedom and justice proclaimed in the first ten amendments of the Constitution."

While the celebration of National Freedom Day springs from the movement to free Negro Americans legally from slavery, it should be noted also that the Thirteenth Amendment prohibits the enforced labor of any American people. As the United States Supreme Court has declared, "If Mexican peonage or the Chinese coolie labor system shall develop slavery of the Mexican or Chinese race within our territory, this Amendment may be safely trusted to make it void. And so if other rights are assailed by the states which properly and necessarily fall within the protection of these articles, that protection will apply, though the party interested may not be of African descent."

This day observing the adoption of the Thirteenth Amendment is a significant step in the history of American liberty. The amendment is one of the historic provisions of the Constitution which binds the federal government, the states, and all persons within the nation. The United States Supreme Court has upheld the power of Congress under the Thirteenth Amendment to maintain the freedom which it has proclaimed. Indirect programs of compulsory labor and service have been declared in violation of the amendment, as cases have been brought before the Supreme Court. No attempt has been made in a direct way by any state legislature or Congress to nullify the provisions of this amendment. National Freedom Day signifies the physical freedom from enslavement or oppression in our country of peoples of any race, color, or other grouping.

ABRAHAM LINCOLN'S BIRTHDAY

(*February 12*)

TREVOR N. DUPUY

"Now HE BELONGS to the ages."

So spoke Secretary of War Edwin M. Stanton, as he gazed sorrowfully at the lifeless body of President Abraham Lincoln at 7:30 A.M., Saturday, April 15, 1865. Shortly after 10:00 P.M. the previous evening, the President, sitting beside Mrs. Lincoln, had been watching a play at Ford's Theater in Washington, when John Wilkes Booth crept into the box to shoot him in the back of the head. The wound had been mortal, and Lincoln never regained consciousness; yet for more than nine hours his stout heart had vainly tried to keep a spark of life in his body. But the shallow breathing had stopped; the heart was still. The President of the United States was dead.

Stanton's words were more prophetic than he realized. For Abraham Lincoln, more than any other American, belongs to the world as well as to the ages—admired, loved, and respected by people of all faiths, races, and political beliefs everywhere.

In our own country, Lincoln stands with George Washington in national esteem and affection. Washington, more than any other man, had helped to establish the United States and to provide it with a new and viable government; Lincoln, more than any other, preserved the United States as a single nation under one government and one flag. All of

23

us are drawn to Lincoln, the homely man of the people, because of his warmth, humility, and kindness—qualities which sometimes cause us to overlook the intellectual brilliance, moral courage, and steely determination that made him truly great.

Abraham Lincoln was born on February 12, 1809, in an isolated log cabin in the woods of central Kentucky. Seven years later his father, Thomas Lincoln, moved the family to southwestern Indiana, where Abraham spent his childhood and helped his father eke out a sparse living from their frontier farm. His parents could neither read nor write, and young "Abe" probably spent no more than one year in school. But he had a will to learn, particularly to read. There are many tales—some of which are probably imaginary—about how he would walk for miles to borrow a book, or how after a hard day of farm chores he would read by the flickering light of the cabin's open fireplace.

Lincoln grew up to be a tall, strong, raw-boned youth, capable as a plowman and all-round farmer; he was particularly noted for the skill with which he could wield an ax when splitting rails for frontier fences. When he was nineteen, he worked his way to New Orleans and back as a flatboatman on the Ohio and Mississippi rivers. In 1830, at the age of twenty-one, Lincoln and his family moved to a new farm in Illinois. Abraham helped his father clear the land, splitting rails to build fences around the property. But Abe had already decided that he did not want to be a farmer.

Striking off on his own, he settled in New Salem, Illinois, where he worked as a storekeeper, postmaster, and surveyor. Later he enlisted in the local militia unit to fight in the Black Hawk War (1832) and was elected captain of his company —the first indication of his political and leadership abilities. His unit never saw action against the Indians, and Lincoln soon returned to civilian life.

His election to military command had apparently whetted Abe's appetite for political life. After one failure, he was elected to the Illinois state assembly. While serving as a legislator, he studied law and passed the bar examinations in 1836. Early success in law practice in New Salem caused him to move, in 1837, to Springfield, the state capital, where legal opportunities were greater. He continued to be successful, making a considerable local reputation both as a lawyer and as a state legislator, noted for shrewdness, common sense, fairness, and honesty.

In 1842, after a long courtship, Lincoln married Mary Todd, who came from a distinguished Kentucky family and who had met Abraham while she was visiting relatives in Springfield. The Lincolns had four children, all boys; of these only one—Robert Todd—lived to manhood. (The tragedy of her children's deaths, and the horrible experience of having her husband murdered at her side, caused Mary Todd Lincoln to suffer recurrent fits of insanity before she died in 1882.)

Lincoln was a member of the Whig Party and was elected to Congress in 1846. He served only one term, since the decline of the Whig Party and his own criticisms of the Polk Administration's conduct of the Mexican War had made him unpopular in his congressional district. He returned gladly to his profitable law practice in Springfield. For several years he stayed out of politics, but in 1856 he joined the new Republican Party and soon became the leading Republican in Illinois.

In 1858, Lincoln ran for the United States Senate against Democratic Senator Stephen Arnold Douglas, a renowned politician and orator, popularly known as "the Little Giant." In a series of sparkling debates during the election campaign, Lincoln gained national repute. The principal issue of the Lincoln-Douglas debates was whether or not slavery should be allowed in the sparsely settled territories west of the Mississippi River. At that time Lincoln was not advocating the end of slavery in the Southern states where it was already established, but he was opposed to its extension to the newer regions of the West. It was during this campaign that he made his famous, prophetic statement: " 'A house divided against itself cannot stand.' * I believe this government cannot endure permanently half slave and half free."

Lincoln lost a close election to Douglas, but his brilliant performance against one of the nation's leading politicians led to his nomination as the Republican candidate for President in 1860. The Democratic Party was badly divided over the issues of slavery and states' rights, and so Lincoln was opposed in the election not only by Douglas—the official Democratic Party candidate—but also by three Southern Democrats. Thanks to this Democratic split, Lincoln won a clear-cut victory.

Largely because of Lincoln's reputation as an antislavery man, shortly after his election South Carolina seceded, or withdrew, from the United States. Six other Southern states followed and formed the Confederate States of America. When Lincoln was inaugurated President, on March 4, 1861, he was faced with armed rebellion against the authority of the United States.

Lincoln had the terrible choice of accepting the division of the country peacefully and permanently or of reuniting the nation forcefully with probable bloodshed. But although he appealed for harmony and peace, he made clear his conviction that his oath of office demanded that he preserve the Union as a single nation and that he sustain the power of the government in all of the states. Despite his cautious maneuvers to preserve governmental authority, while at the same time attempting to find a compromise solution that the Southern states would accept, war broke out on April 12, 1861, when Confederate troops opened fire on the Union garrison at Fort Sumter, in Charleston Harbor.

There followed four long, terrible years of war. The people of the Confederacy were convinced of the justice of their cause and fought bravely to gain their independence. The Northerners, inspired by Lincoln's leadership, were equally convinced of the justice of the Union cause. For nearly

* If a house be divided against itself, that house cannot stand. (Mark 3:25)

three years, the grim, bloody struggle was a stalemate. Despite an effective Union naval blockade of the South and the gradual conquest of most of the Mississippi Valley, Union armies in the east suffered defeat after defeat at the hands of the brilliant Confederate General Robert E. Lee and his magnificent Army of Northern Virginia.

During this period, Lincoln mastered the problems of the political direction of a great nation in a bitter war. But he had trouble in directing the actual fighting. Seemingly he vacillated between exercising insufficient control over the Union army's generals on the one hand, and trying to direct the details of the campaigns from the White House on the other. Actually he was learning about military affairs. Despite his short service in the Black Hawk War, he knew little about the army. At the same time he was applying his keen, practical intellect to the difficulties of organizing victory with a nation and an army which had been totally unprepared for a major war. And he was fitting his methods to the capabilities and the weaknesses of the generals who led that army—generals who at first seemed to be far less skilled than Southern leaders such as Robert E. Lee and Joseph E. Johnston.

Military matters were not Lincoln's only concern during the war. Carefully but deliberately he set about removing one of the basic causes of the war by ending slavery. On January 1, 1863, he issued his famous Emancipation Proclamation, declaring freedom for some three million Negro slaves in the rebellious states. Still moving cautiously, and with great political skill, two years later he brought about the adoption of the Thirteenth Amendment to the Constitution, which abolished slavery forever in this country.

Lincoln considered that his greatest responsibility during the war was to hold the Northern people together so as to assure the success of the war and the earliest possible reestablishment of a single Union. He did this in many ways: by skillful political maneuvering; by firm and inflexible assertion of the authority of the government when necessary;

27

and by brilliant oratory which gripped the hearts and imagination of the people. One of his greatest successes was the short, simple address which he made at Gettysburg, on November 19, 1863, for the dedication of the cemetery where the dead of the Battle of Gettysburg were buried. This was one of the noblest documents ever written by man, and it apparently was delivered with simple eloquence.

By the end of 1863, Lincoln had learned how to direct national strategy with a brilliance matched by few other civilian leaders in history. He had also learned the limits of his own ability to direct battles while trying to govern the nation. Furthermore, he had found a general who understood the nature and strategy of a vast continental war as well as he did—Ulysses S. Grant, whom he made General in Chief of all the Union armies.

Lincoln's faith in Grant never faltered, even during the costly battles of 1864 in Virginia, where Grant and Lee—two of the greatest military leaders of American history—fought each other to a standstill. Finally, after the winter-long siege of Richmond and Petersburg, Grant overwhelmed Lee's starving army at Appomattox, then granted Lee magnanimous surrender terms.

Lincoln approved these terms. As the rest of the crumbling Southern armies began to surrender, he prepared for a period of adjustment in which the economically prostrate South would be helped to recover, and the recently freed Negroes— few of whom had had a chance for any education—would also be helped to take their proper place as full-fledged, responsible citizens.

But, only five days after Appomattox, the gun of John Wilkes Booth brought these plans to an end. The country still suffers from the terrible consequences of that assassination and of the regional and racial bitterness resulting from the Reconstruction period which followed, when heedless Northerners took out their wrath on the South for having started the war. And although Southerners had not been responsible, this Reconstruction was also vengeance for the death of Abraham Lincoln by men of little tolerance, understanding, and intelligence, who had inherited from him the responsibility for reestablishing the Southern states in the Union.

Many farsighted Southerners foresaw these consequences when they learned of the President's murder. General Joseph E. Johnston, who heard about the tragedy when he surrendered to General Sherman, told Sherman that this was "the greatest possible calamity to the South since Lincoln was the South's best friend in the federal government." Lee, who admitted that the "benignity and goodness of Lincoln" had influenced his surrender as much as Grant's guns, said that he regretted the death as much as any Northerner could.

These were tributes from men who had been Lincoln's bitterest and most determined foes; tributes to a man of honor, a man of wisdom, a man of strength, and a man of compassionate magnanimity.

When he became President, Lincoln had been ridiculed as a country bumpkin by cultured political and social leaders of the northeast and southern states. Even members of his own Cabinet were at first contemptuous of this lanky, awkward, homely frontier lawyer. Many Northerners had thought that he should have backed down and let the Confederate states go their own way without war, and they bitterly attacked him, some even up to the time of his death. And many more vocal critics appeared during the war, when brilliant Southern military leadership—and some serious Union blunders—caused the war to continue seemingly without end.

Yet slowly, surely, it became evident to those close to the President, and eventually to the entire country, that this was a man of exceptional ability and strength; a superb politician who never forgot the ultimate interests of the nation. This was also a man who could patiently work with and through lesser men to accomplish his purposes and at the same time gain the votes that were essential if he were to win the war and the peace that followed. He was a man who could take jibes and cruel criticism without rancor, who never lost his sense of humor or his ability to tell funny stories—jokes often designed to correct gently a subordinate's error or to support sagging spirits in times of crisis or calamity.

This was the man who epitomized then, as he does today, the virtues of the American concept of freedom and democracy. This was the man who freed the slaves, the man who dedicated himself and his countrymen—and all freedom-loving men of good will everywhere—not only to "the proposition that all men are created equal," but also to the firm resolve "that this nation, under God, shall have a new birth of freedom; and that government of the people, by the people, for the people, shall not perish from the earth."

GEORGE WASHINGTON'S BIRTHDAY

(February 22)

GAY M. HAMMERMAN

WASHINGTON'S BIRTHDAY is celebrated with cherry pies and paper hatchets—and with speeches of reverence and gratitude. Both ways of honoring the first President of the United States are appropriate. He is America's great founding hero, and symbols and folklore have grown up around great folk heroes throughout history. We know now that young George never used his new hatchet on his father's cherry tree, and therefore he could not have confessed to the deed. Yet this story has real meaning. It was made up by Parson Weems, a lively clergyman and book peddler who wanted to dramatize the well-known fact—for which there was ample, but less colorful, evidence—that Washington was an exceptionally brave and honest man.

Most children know Washington's face. They know, at least, his face as it appears on the dollar bill and on many schoolroom walls. These portraits are very dignified—and lifeless. They are reproductions of paintings made when Washington was an old man, and when dignity and reserve had become two of his most striking characteristics. His tremendous vitality had been worn down by illness and by many years of intense, full-time work for his country. Homely physical details added to their stiffness; at least one portrait painter packed cotton around Washington's ill-fitting

31

false teeth in an attempt to give a more natural fullness to his face.

It is unfortunate that some of the earlier portraits of Washington are not more often seen, and that we have no picture of him as a young man of twenty-one. He had brown hair then, and although his skin was scarred from smallpox, his blue-gray eyes were set in a face much more handsome than those of the familiar pictures. He was a tall, big-boned man, about 6 feet 3 inches, who had huge, strong hands and wore size thirteen boots. He spent much time on horseback and rode magnificently.

Washington was born on a farm in Westmoreland County, Virginia, on February 11, 1732, and February 11 was his birthday until he was twenty, when a change in the calendar made the date February 22. George's father was a fairly well-to-do man who owned several farms and an iron furnace. He had four sons and daughters younger than George and also three older children by his first wife. George's family was broken by his father's death when George was eleven, but the pleasant farm life continued. He finished school at fourteen with the equivalent of a good eighth-grade education and then learned to survey land, probably taught by a friendly neighbor, using old instruments of his father's. Although many American leaders of his time went to college, Washington never did.

When he was sixteen, George went to live with his married half brother Lawrence at Mount Vernon, a handsome white house on the Potomac River. He met the prominent Fairfax family, who lived nearby. Old Lord Fairfax owned at least a million acres of land stretching far into the western mountains of Virginia. Not sure just where his boundaries lay, Fairfax sent George on a surveying trip with young George William Fairfax. They crossed the mountains on horseback, sometimes camping out at night. Soon George was making his living as a surveyor and buying some of the best land for himself.

Lawrence, whom George looked up to as a second father, died of tuberculosis when George was twenty, and left him

32

Mount Vernon. Thus by the time he was twenty-one, Washington was a prosperous and promising young man.

George also took Lawrence's place as a leader of the Virginia militia, the volunteer citizen-soldiers of the colony. He immediately volunteered to carry a message from the British governor of Virginia to the French commander in the Ohio River area far to the west. Washington's mission required a long winter journey on horseback through wild country. When he returned, he reported that the French planned to occupy the whole area, which was claimed by the British, and in the spring of 1754 Governor Robert Dinwiddie sent Washington and about four hundred men to reinforce a fort on the present site of Pittsburgh.

Before he reached the fort, Washington learned that the French had already seized it, and renamed it Duquesne; but he pressed forward, met an advance party of French, and defeated them. Washington did not receive adequate reinforcements to hold off the French after this victory, and a little fort he hastily built was not strong enough to do so. Although he was defeated, he had gained both experience and reputation as a fighter.

The next year he accompanied British General Edward Braddock in another attempt to take Fort Duquesne. Braddock's red-coated troops were ambushed by the French and Indians, Braddock was killed, and Washington, although sick with dysentery, rallied the survivors and helped lead them to safety. Partly as a result, he was made commander of the entire Virginia militia at the young age of twenty-three. He spent the next few years using his small body of troops to protect the settlers along the whole Virginia frontier, as best he could, from attacks by hostile Indians. He was also present when Fort Duquesne was finally captured from the French.

The fifteen years between the French and Indian War and the Revolution were Washington's happiest. He resigned his commission near the end of 1758, returned to Mount Vernon, and in January, 1759, married the petite and charming Martha Dandridge Custis, a widow and the wealthiest woman in Virginia. Martha had two young children, and Washington, who never was to have children of his own, loved and indulged little "Patsy" (Martha) and "Jackie" (John). Farming, which he called a "delectable occupation," was his great joy. The work was done by Negro slaves, as on all large Virginia farms then, but Washington supervised every detail and often took off his coat and showed how a particular job should be done. During this period he also became active in politics. After two defeats, he was elected to the Virginia House of Burgesses, forerunner of the state legislature.

Washington was in the House of Burgesses in 1765 when Patrick Henry made a stirring speech against the British Stamp Act—a law which many Americans felt levied taxes illegally. Washington agreed, but made no speeches; he never learned to address a group easily and was often at a loss for words when his opinion was suddenly asked at a meeting.

During the next decade, as relations with England worsened, Washington made clear his sympathy with the American patriots, and in 1774 and 1775 he was elected to the Continental Congress in Philadelphia. When the Second Continental Congress met in May, 1775, the first shots of the Revolutionary War had been fired in Massachusetts, and Washington wore his Virginia militia uniform.

A general for the American armies was needed. Washington was chosen, partly because of his reputation for military skill and sound judgment, and partly because it was felt that a Virginian could best unify the Colonies' effort. Most of the leaders had until then come from Massachusetts, since that was where the first clashes had taken place. Washington knew, and said, that he was not fully qualified; he had never commanded large numbers of men nor directed operations on anything approaching a continental scale. But he realized that his colleagues honestly thought him the best man for the job, so he accepted it, refused to take any pay, and promised to do his best.

George Washington's Birthday

The Revolutionary War was basically a defensive war for the Americans. Although the British had much more money and equipment, many more trained men, and the world's greatest navy, their home base was far away. If they could be held off long enough, Washington believed that the Colonies could win. His task was to keep his small forces of volunteers together, train them as soldiers, keep them clothed and fed, lift their hopes with whatever victories he could win, and inspire them with his devotion to their common cause. In July, 1776, this cause became freedom—independence from Britain.

Washington and his men first heard the words of the Declaration of Independence in New York, where they were trying to hold the city on orders from the Congress. From then until Christmas night, Washington fought one long series of battles and retreats—across Long Island Sound, up Manhattan Island, and through New Jersey. He knew that mistakes of his had helped the British—trying to hold an impossible position, failure to check on important details, inadequately protecting his plans from British spies. He never made such mistakes again. He supervised every aspect of the retreats personally. He was the last man in the last boat that left the Brooklyn shore for Manhattan. As he led the men through New Jersey, he himself destroyed bridges behind them and cut trees as obstacles to the pursuing British. Then, in December, when the war seemed lost, he decided to attack.

On Christmas night, 1776, Washington ferried his men across the partly frozen Delaware River. Attacking Trenton, New Jersey, he took its defenders by surprise. His men marched and fought in falling sleet, without overcoats, many without shoes. It was a complete victory. They returned a few days later, to win again at Princeton. Here, as he often did, Washington personally led his soldiers, exposing himself to enemy fire. Letters from his men tell how much it meant to see their leader, tall in the saddle, sharing their danger.

These victories boosted morale, and after another year of

fighting, and a terrible winter of hardship at Valley Forge, Pennsylvania, the tide turned. France became America's ally, and the hungry, ragged fighters of Valley Forge had been trained into a real army.

The Americans, with French help, continued to hold off the British for four more years, and in 1781 Washington forced the surrender of Lord Cornwallis at Yorktown, Virginia. Yorktown caused the British to abandon the struggle and to grant independence to the United States.

After the success of the Revolution, Washington returned to his Virginia home, where he hoped to spend the rest of his life. But in the confusion and turmoil of the early years of independence, his fellow citizens turned again to him for leadership. He presided over the Constitutional Convention of 1787 and worked for ratification of the new Constitution. The new government called for a President of the United States—and Washington was the electors' unanimous choice.

Inaugurated on April 30, 1789, Washington served two terms. He understood thoroughly the importance of his office, and was conscious that everything he did set precedents for the future. With his sound judgment, inflexible integrity, and great prestige, he erected a solid foundation on which the young country could grow. At home, he established the supremacy of the federal government, built a sound currency system, solidified the nation's credit, and took steps to protect and develop the infant American industries. Abroad, he followed a course free from involvement in Europe's quarrels, established the nation's western borders by a series of treaties, and set sound precedents for the role of the President in the conduct of American foreign policy.

A strong executive who shunned the excesses of power, he was a skillful administrator and an influential political leader. Not always able to maintain harmony among divergent elements, he held himself above partisanship and balanced opposing views as best he could. If he favored one side, it was that which sought to strengthen the authority of the national government. He had learned during the Revolutionary War to choose and use his assistants well, and as President he set up a Cabinet of advisers—one of the precedents that his successors have followed. When he retired from office, he urged his countrymen in his Farewell Address to support the nation and its Constitution, to avoid factional disputes, and to beware of permanent foreign alliances. He died on December 14, 1799, beloved and mourned by the nation and the world.

The celebration of Washington's Birthday is a fitting reminder of his crucial importance to our nation—that he gained our freedom from England, helped establish our Constitution, and proved that strong executive power is consistent with government by the people. Washington truly deserves to be called the "Father of His Country." Without him, the United States could hardly have begun. He is a man unequaled in our history as a fighter and as a builder.

ALAMO DAY

(*March 6*)

WALTER RUNDELL, JR.

THE LEGACY of the famous San Antonio fort, the Alamo, which is especially recalled each March 6 in Texas, is manifold. It is not the collapse of the Alamo that we commemorate on Alamo Day, but rather the Alamo as a symbol. Like Lexington and Concord, it is a spot where heroes stood and died for freedom—where men were willing to give their lives so that others could be free to govern themselves. The Alamo, as a psychological symbol, was defeat spawning victory. It was a massacre to be avenged.

American settlement of Texas began in 1821 when Stephen F. Austin brought his first colonists into the vast northern province of the newly independent Mexico. Working in strict compliance with the stipulations of the Mexican government, Austin established a successful colony. Other *empresarios,* as the colonizers were called, included David G. Burnet, Haden Edwards, and Benjamin R. Milam. But colonization in Texas was not the exclusive concern of Americans; among the prominent Mexican *empresarios* were Alonso de León and Lorenzo de Zavala.

The Americans who came to Texas naturally brought with them their own traditions and culture. This culture soon came in sharp conflict with that of the Mexicans. Colonizers could understand and accept the requirement that they be-

38

come Mexican citizens; but they had difficulty reconciling themselves to the government's religious pronouncements, which specified that only the Roman Catholic Church could conduct services and that the new residents of Texas could not engage in any other organized form of worship. Additionally, when the Mexican government frowned on slavery, the colonists were greatly alarmed, for most of them had emigrated from the Southern states and expected to re-create that institution in their new home.

Instability marked the early years of the Mexican republic. The constitution adopted in 1824 provided for a federal government, with Coahuila-Texas as one unit. Within this unit, Texas had one (later two) of the twelve representatives in the legislature. Not only did Texas feel underrepresented, but they also felt neglected, since the capital in Saltillo was far away. Nevertheless, the 1824 constitution provided a republican type of government. In Mexico, however, there was no tradition of republicanism, and representative government had no roots. Power soon gravitated into the hands of the greedy and strong.

No man in Mexican history has come to symbolize political opportunism more than General Antonio López de Santa Anna. Although a series of revolutions found Santa Anna's fortunes varying, in 1832 he came to power as a liberal. Professing great faith in the reform constitution, he proclaimed: "I swear to you that I oppose all efforts aimed at destruction of the constitution and that I would die before accepting any other power than that designated by it." By 1834, Santa Anna was convinced that he had amassed sufficient power to discard the 1824 constitution and establish his dictatorship. The federal nature of the government succumbed to his centralized control.

Among Santa Anna's determinations was to keep the refractory Texans in line. Antagonisms between the government and the Texas colonists were long standing. Haden Edwards had led the abortive Fredonian Rebellion in 1825, and insurgents had besieged the Mexican fort at Anahuac in

1832 and again in 1835. It was evident that the thousands of Americans who had poured into Texas and who outnumbered the native Mexicans 10 to 1 would some day reestablish their ties with the United States, rather than continue under a Mexican rule which they found offensive. Moreover, the American government maintained its active interest in Texas, Andrew Jackson offering $5,000,000 for the territory. With all signs pointing to a revolt in Texas, Santa Anna renewed his vows to maintain control.

To quell any insurrection, Santa Anna sent a cavalry detachment into Texas. When the force reached Gonzales on October 2, 1835, and demanded surrender of the town's cannon, it was answered with a spirited attack. The fleeing Mexican soldiers gave notice through the countryside that the Texas Revolution had begun. The Texans thought that San Antonio, in Bexar County, would be a key outpost of defense against Santa Anna. Calling for volunteers to take the town, the patriot Ben Milam asked: "Who'll go to Bexar with old Ben Milam?" His force took the settlement on December 5. The Texans realized that in the face of Santa Anna's approaching army, the position which they could best defend was the abandoned mission, San Antonio de Valero, popularly known as the Alamo. The name came from Alamo de Parras, Mexico, headquarters of a colonial company that once maintained an office in the mission.

Commanding the regulars in the Alamo was Colonel William B. Travis; Jim Bowie commanded the volunteers, who boasted Davy Crockett among their ranks. Command fell upon Travis when Bowie became too ill to function. As the men prepared their fortress for a siege, news filtered through of Santa Anna's approaching army. He reached San Antonio on February 23, 1836, and began the attack on the Alamo. The Mexican army of 2,400 faced a defending force of some 150 Texans (32 men from Gonzales joined the garrison on March 1). From the beginning the Texans knew defeat was inevitable.

The next day came Travis' famous appeal "To the People

of Texas and all Americans in the World." ". . . I shall never surrender or retreat. Then I call on you, in the name of liberty, of patriotism, and of everything dear to the American character, to come to our aid with all dispatch. . . ." In a later letter Travis said that if Texas' independence were declared, he and his troops—and the world—would understand what they were fighting for. Although Travis never learned it, the Texas Declaration of Independence was signed at Washington, on the Brazos River, on March 2, 1836, as the Mexican forces continued to assault the Alamo.

The final push came in the early hours of March 6, with the band playing the sinister *Degüello,* a Spanish march signifying battle to the death. The valiant defenders of the Alamo fought well. But they were crushed by the numerical superiority of the Mexicans. All 182 combatants in the Alamo perished in the fray, taking with them approximately 600 Mexicans. Because all the defenders died in the Alamo, it was popularly said, "Thermopylae had its messenger of defeat—the Alamo had none." There were, however, many people who left the Alamo during the siege. The most famous of those was Mrs. Susannah Dickinson, widow of a slain defender, who endured the entire battle and was released by the Mexicans.

If defense of the Alamo was futile from the outset, what did it accomplish? Most important, it delayed Santa Anna's advance into Texas for two weeks. No one pretended that the force at the Alamo represented the main strength of the Texas army. That lay to the east with General Sam Houston. The two-week delay enabled General Houston, commander-in-chief of the Texas forces, to assemble his men and prepare for battle. News of the heroes' stand at the Alamo also solidified public opinion in Texas and gave the Americans new will to win. And the Alamo had given the Texas forces their battle cry. On April 21, when Sam Houston's army charged down upon the Mexicans at San Jacinto, they were shouting, "Remember the Alamo!" The total victory at San Jacinto, which included the capture of Santa Anna, secured the independence of Texas. From that point on, Texas citizens would be able to govern themselves, as Americans were bound to do.

While the heritage of the Alamo is usually considered in terms of its meaning to all Americans, it has a special message for Mexican-Americans. Seven of the valiant men who gave their lives in the Alamo on March 6, 1836, were Mexicans. Hence Americans of Mexican descent can take pride in the fact that some of their forebears sacrificed their lives for the principle of self-government. The defense of the Alamo represents opposition to dictatorial tyranny in the person of Santa Anna. Such tyranny later became just as unbearable to the Mexicans he ruled, and they overthrew him. Thus the battle at the Alamo did not pit Mexicans against Texans, as such, but rather tyranny against freedom.

PAN-AMERICAN DAY

(April 14)

WILLIAM MANGER

SOUTH OF THE United States, in Central America, South America, and among the islands of the Caribbean, are twenty countries which, with the United States, form the Pan-American family of nations. *Pan* is a Greek word meaning "all," and Pan America thus means *all* America—the twenty-one Americas. These countries are joined together in an association which is now called the Organization of American States (OAS), an organization similar in many respects to the United Nations.

In 1930, the representatives of these twenty-one countries proposed that April 14 be an annual day of celebration in all the countries, as a symbol of their membership in one great continental community. Since that time, the President of the United States has each year issued a proclamation setting aside April 14 as Pan-American Day and calling upon our people to observe the day with appropriate ceremonies. The governors and mayors of many states and municipalities also issue similar proclamations, covering the observance not only of Pan-American Day but of the entire week in which the day falls.

Similar action is taken in each of the other twenty countries. Pan-American Day, thus, is not merely a national but an international anniversary observed in all the countries that are members of the Organization of American States:

43

Argentina, Bolivia, Brazil, Chile, Colombia, Costa Rica, Cuba,* Dominican Republic, Ecuador, El Salvador, Guatemala, Haiti, Honduras, Mexico, Nicaragua, Panama, Paraguay, Peru, the United States, Uruguay, and Venezuela.

In the eighteen Spanish-speaking countries, Pan-American Day is observed as "Día de las Americas"; in Portuguese-speaking Brazil as "Dia Pan-Americano"; and in French-speaking Haiti as "Le Jour des Amériques."

April 14 was chosen as the date for this continental anniversary because it was on that date, in 1890, that the resolution creating the Pan-American Union was adopted at the First Pan-American Conference held in Washington. This marked the beginning of the Pan-American movement as it exists today, a movement that includes all the independent nations of the Western Hemisphere. Other dates were considered, but a further reason for selecting April 14 was that schools are in session in nearly all the American republics in April, and the framers of the resolution were particularly anxious to select a date that could be observed by schoolchildren.

The United States and the other countries that make up this Pan-American family have much in common. In the years immediately following the discovery of America by Columbus, all regions of North and South America were colonies of European powers. When the United States declared its independence of Britain in 1776, it inspired the peoples of Latin America also to seek their independence from Spain and Portugal. This they did early in the nineteenth century under the leadership of a number of colonial patriots. Principal among these were Simón Bolívar, "the Liberator," who is frequently called "the George Washington of South America," for he was instrumental in liberating five of the present-day republics of South America;** José de San

---

* In 1961, the Cuban regime of Fidel Castro was suspended from the OAS because of its association with communism. The Cuban nation and people, however, continue to be considered a part of the Pan-American family.
** Colombia, Venezuela, Peru, Ecuador, and Bolivia.

Martín, the national hero of Argentina; José Artigas of Uruguay; and Bernardo O'Higgins of Chile (Spanish, in spite of his Irish name).

Again following the example of the United States, all these countries eventually adopted the democratic republican form of government, and they used the Constitution of the United States as a model in setting up their governments. It is understandable, therefore, that long ago a close understanding developed among the peoples and governments of the American republics, and that they decided to join together and cooperate with one another. The idea of forming a Pan-American association of nations was, in fact, originally suggested as far back as 1826 by Simón Bolívar.

The Pan-American system, or the Organization of American States (OAS), is the oldest system of international relations in the world. It is unique in that all the member states are on a level of complete equality with one another. There are large states and small states, strong states and weak states; but each has only one vote, and the vote of the smallest and weakest is equal to that of the largest and strongest. The United States with its population of 189,000,-000, and Brazil with an area larger even than that of the continental United States, each have one vote, as do Costa Rica, with a population of about one million, and Uruguay, with an area only equal to that of some of the smaller states of the United States. There is no veto in the Organization of American States.

Like the United Nations, the OAS has as its first and primary objective the preserving of peace. In contrast to other parts of the world, the Western Hemisphere has been remarkably free from international wars, particularly since the establishment of the OAS. When differences arise between two or more states, the OAS, either through its permanent Council or the Inter-American Peace Committee, seeks a peaceful settlement. In the event of aggression by one state against another, the OAS may, and has, applied sanctions in order to deter or punish the aggressor. Since the close of World War II, at least ten cases have been submitted to the OAS, most of them involving the smaller countries of Central America and the Caribbean. The measures taken in these cases have usually been successful.

In recent years the American republics have become seriously concerned by the activities of international communism in the Western Hemisphere. This first presented problems in Guatemala in 1954; the threat assumed more serious proportions when Fidel Castro came to power in Cuba in 1959 and then associated himself with the Soviet bloc. When Russia attempted to place missiles in Cuba in 1962, as a threat to the United States, the countries of the OAS admirably demonstrated their support for the United States by agreeing that all measures to remove the missiles should be taken, including the use of force, *if necessary*. In April, 1965, the junta government of the Dominican Republic was overthrown by rebel forces. The United States, fearing a Communist takeover, sent 30,000 American troops to Santo Domingo. This action violated the OAS charter, and the U.S. was criticized by many nations for its unilateral intervention. But soon after, the OAS sent in its own multination peace-keeping force and negotiations between the junta government and the rebels were begun.

It is obvious to most people in the Pan-American Union that the danger communism presents to Latin America can best be met by solving the difficult economic and social problems of these countries. Most of the Latin-American members of the OAS are considered among the underdeveloped countries of the world. Their people have a low standard of living and a high rate of illiteracy; there is a lack of housing, health, and sanitation facilities. To help meet these needs, the United States is rendering assistance under the Alliance for Progress. And within the OAS, the Inter-American Development Bank, the Pan-American Health Organization, the Inter-American Agricultural Institute, and other OAS agencies, all are carrying out programs in the different countries to help solve these problems and thereby strengthen the forces of democracy.

The principal activities of the OAS are centered in the

beautiful Pan-American Union Building in Washington with its typically Spanish-American style of architecture. In the patio, or interior court, an Aztec fountain bubbles amidst tropical plants, a banana tree, and a coffee tree; a sliding glass roof admits rain and sun in the summer and keeps out snow and sleet in the winter. Its style is distinct from that of the other public buildings of the nation's capital.

On the second floor is the great Hall of the Americas where Pan-American conferences, including meetings of the Ministers of Foreign Affairs and other functions, are held. In this building also is the assembly hall of the Council of the OAS, a permanent board of representatives from each of the member states, which is in continuous session supervising and directing much of the work of the OAS. Each chair bears the name and the coat-of-arms of the country whose representative occupies it.

When the Pan-American system was originally set up in 1890, it functioned within the framework of a Union of American *Republics*. In 1948, however, the name Organization of American *States* was adopted, to open the door for the admission of other self-governing states that might emerge in the Western Hemisphere. Canada, Jamaica, and Trinidad-Tobago now have self-governing status, and all have expressed interest in possible membership in the OAS. In fact, although Canada is not yet a member, in the basement of the Pan-American Union Building in Washington there is a chair with the name of Canada and the Canadian seal in the expectation that Canada will some day join the organization. Other European possessions in the Western Hemisphere, as they become self-governing, may be expected to do likewise.

The Organization of American States, which has patterned its quest for independence and free democratic government after the United States, contributes to peace, freedom, and prosperity not only throughout the Western Hemisphere but throughout the world. Therefore, April 14 has been set aside as a special day for all citizen members to strengthen their common desire for lasting cooperation.

PATRIOTS' DAY

(April 19)

CHARLES B. MACDONALD

By the rude bridge that arched the flood,
Their flag to April's breeze unfurled,
Here once the embattled farmers stood,
And fired the shot heard round the world.

RALPH WALDO EMERSON wrote these words about a skirmish that took place near a little white bridge, at Concord, Massachusetts, on April 19, 1775. The Revolutionary War had begun. On that day, a small band of patriotic colonists, inexperienced in methods of war, fought desperately for the freedom which we now enjoy. Each year, on April 19, certain states proclaim a holiday to commemorate "Patriots' Day."

For more than ten years, resentment had been growing among the colonists in America. To people long accustomed to conducting their own affairs with a minimum of interference from the mother country, it was difficult to discern any reason for the restrictive measures imposed by the government of King George III. Few would deny that new responsibilities brought about by victory in the Seven Years' War and expansion of the British Empire would cost money; but the colonists considered they already were paying their share. There was little acceptance of the argument that much of the new revenue would be used to help defray the

48

costs of British garrisons stationed on the Colonial frontiers to keep the Indians quiet. To the colonists, there no longer seemed to be need for this expensive protection.

It was the Stamp Act of 1765 around which American resentment began to crystallize. The act, which provided for revenue stamps to be affixed to newspapers, licenses, commercial bills, various legal documents, and other official and semiofficial papers, produced prompt and sometimes violent reaction, including an effective boycott of British goods. The colonists claimed that the British Parliament had no authority to impose taxes on them so long as they had no representatives in Parliament. The issue was: "Taxation without representation."

Prompted by the presumed injustices of the Stamp Act, nine of the thirteen Colonies sent delegates to a Congress which met in New York in October, 1765. This was the first full inter-Colonial meeting, on Colonial initiative, and can be considered the first formal step of the Colonies to act together as one.

The implications of this Congress were lost on the government of George III, although Parliament repealed the Stamp Act anyway, primarily because of pressure from English businessmen damaged by the boycott. But at the same time, Parliament passed a Declaration Act affirming sweeping powers of sovereignty over the Colonies.

In the general amicability that followed repeal of the Stamp Act, the broad implications of the Declaration Act passed almost unnoticed. But not for long. The so-called Townshend Acts, named after a new Prime Minister in George III's government, imposed a customs tax on several commodities, including tea. Resentment flared again and grew in intensity when the British government granted the powerful East India Company a monopoly on the importation of tea to the Colonies. Some colonists pictured dire consequences from this monopoly. Their agitation culminated in the famous Boston Tea Party of December 16, 1773, when a band of men disguised as Indians boarded three ships loaded with tea in Boston Harbor and dumped the cargoes into the water.

News of the Boston Tea Party inflamed opinion on both sides of the Atlantic. In England, it led to passage of what became known in America as the "Intolerable Acts," a series of punitive laws that included a provision for closing the port of Boston until the scuttled tea was paid for. Rallying to Massachusetts' side, all the Colonies formed unauthorized popular assemblies, and on September 5, 1774, twelve of them sent delegates to Philadelphia for the First Continental Congress. Their objective was "to consult upon the present unhappy state of the Colonies."

The Colonies simultaneously began preparations for military resistance. In Massachusetts, where this resistance was destined to be tested first, the Provincial Congress established control over the militia by purging officers with Loyalist sentiments, and then set out to accumulate stores of ammunition and weapons. The major depot for these stores was at Concord, some sixteen miles from Boston.

When the news reached Major General Thomas Gage, the commander of the British garrison in Boston, he readied an expedition of about seven hundred men under Lieutenant Colonel Francis Smith to march to Concord to seize and destroy the military stores. Although General Gage tried to keep his plans secret, the patriots learned of them and two messengers—William Dawes and Paul Revere—left on horseback a few hours ahead of the British to spread the alarm. At Lexington, Dr. Samuel Prescott joined Revere and Dawes, and he got through to Concord after Revere and Dawes were captured. This exploit, on the night of April 18, 1775, later inspired Henry Wadsworth Longfellow to write—with some historical inaccuracy—his patriotic poem, "Paul Revere's Ride."

> *Listen, my children, and you shall hear*
> *Of the midnight ride of Paul Revere . . .*

Patriots' Day

. . . "If the British march
By land or sea from the town to-night,
Hang a lantern aloft in the belfry-arch
Of the North Church tower as a signal light—

One, if by land, and two, if by sea;
And I on the opposite shore will be
Ready to ride and spread the alarm
Through every Middlesex village and farm,
For the country-folk to be up and to arm."

In Lexington, two-thirds of the way to Concord, church bells began to ring before daylight, and some seventy sleepy-eyed men scrambled from their beds to assemble on the village green under Captain Jonas Parker. From over the hills and down the road came the sound of marching men.

The British were coming.

The advance guard of General Gage's detachment under Royal Marine Major Pitcairn reached Lexington at dawn. Confronted by the patriotic minutemen, who seemed in their civilian garb and with their odd assortment of weapons to be only playing soldier, a British officer ordered them to disperse. But the farmers of Lexington stood their ground.

What happened next remains a matter of conjecture, but somebody on one side or the other opened fire. The War for American Independence, the Revolutionary War, had begun. Eight of the colonists were killed, ten more wounded, the remainder put to flight.

Proceeding to Concord, the British soldiers began to destroy such of the military stores that had not already been hidden by the forewarned patriots. Meanwhile a band of about four hundred patriots had gathered on the far side of the Concord River, beyond the little white North Bridge. Advancing, they attacked the outnumbered British bridge guards and "fired the shot heard round the world." Colonel Smith hurried reinforcements to the bridge and repulsed the attack. But worried by the menacing attitude and growing numbers of the patriots, he decided that he had accomplished his mission, and ordered a hasty march back to Boston.

Perhaps dizzied by this apparent success, the patriots at first failed to pursue their advantage. But as more armed civilians gathered along the dusty road to watch the grim soldiers begin their trek back to Boston, a few bold men opened fire. In one of history's early examples of what we now call guerrilla warfare, patriots all along the road back to Boston began to exact their toll of the British soldiers in their bright crimson uniforms. During that long, hot afternoon, the British vainly tried to beat off their tormentors. But the patriots scampered away from each attack, only to return to fire again. In Longfellow's words:

> . . . *From behind each fence and farmyard wall,*
> *Chasing the redcoats down the lane,*
> *Then crossing the fields to emerge again*
> *Under the trees at the turn of the road*
> *And only pausing to fire and load.*

By the time the British returned to Boston, they had lost, out of a total force of over fifteen hundred, nearly three hundred. News of Lexington and Concord burned through the Colonies. Regardless of who had fired the first shot, the British drew the blame, and the colonists stirred to action.

Thus, the events of what was in effect the first Patriots' Day sparked the tinder of American desires for independence. The Revolutionary War had begun!

ARBOR DAY

(Usually late April or early May)

NORMAN A. GRAEBNER

TREE CULTURE has always been a mark of civilization. Long before the discovery of America, Asians and Europeans alike, motivated as much by the beauty as by the usefulness of trees, planted their sacred groves, avenues, roadsides, and walks.

Early colonists planted orchards. And it was the absence of fruit trees that gave rise to the remarkable career of "Johnny Appleseed." This strange New Englander, whose name was John Chapman, roamed alone through Pennsylvania and Ohio in 1797, living on the fringes of pioneer settlements. In his baggage, he carried a pouch of apple seeds.

Chapman would clear a few rods of ground in the forest, surround it with brush fence, and plant his seeds. Twenty miles or so away he would repeat the operation. In this manner he supplied settlers with seedlings, leaving behind him such vivid yarns about his eccentricities that he became a legend in our history.

The traditional tree-planting festival, Arbor Day, grew out of conditions which existed on treeless prairies after mid-nineteenth-century settlers began to encroach on the territory west of the Missouri River, rapidly cutting down the few trees that were there. So serious was the need of these farmers for construction materials—and defense against the winds that swept the plains unhindered—that Kansas provided a tree-bounty law to encourage the planting of trees; Nebraska and Dakota Territory followed. But it was a newspaper editor in Nebraska who championed the idea of systematic tree-planting on a specific day.

In 1855, J. Sterling Morton settled in the tiny village of Nebraska City, Nebraska, and became editor of the Nebraska City *News*. Convinced that the civilization of the prairie states would be limited as long as that region lacked trees, and equally convinced that trees could flourish on the prairies, Morton urged Nebraskans to plant fruit trees as well as forest trees. A leading citizen of his new state, he pleaded the cause:

> *There is beauty in a well-ordered orchard which is a "joy forever." It is a blessing to him who plants it, and it perpetuates his name and memory keeping it fresh as the fruit it bears long after he has ceased to live. . . . If I had the power I would compel every man in the State who had a home of his own, to plant out and cultivate fruit trees.*

At the time Morton gave his address, he was a member of the Nebraska State Board of Agriculture to whom he introduced a resolution "that April 10, 1872, be . . . especially set apart and consecrated for tree planting in the State of Nebraska, and that the State Board of Agriculture hereby names it Arbor Day." The resolution was adopted and prizes were offered to the county agricultural society and to the individual who planted the greatest number of trees. Nebraskans planted over a million trees.

Two years later, Nebraska issued a proclamation calling upon all citizens of the state to celebrate Arbor Day, and later the legislature passed a resolution which termed Nebraska "The Tree Planters' State." Morton himself became Secretary of Agriculture under President Grover Cleveland in 1893, and his gracious mansion, Arbor Lodge, located on a hill outside Nebraska City and surrounded by sixty-five acres of woodlands, is now one of the state's most popular parks.

Efforts to extend the concept of Arbor Day in other states were conducted by agricultural associations or civic authorities. But in Cincinnati, on Ohio's first Arbor Day in 1882, almost twenty thousand schoolchildren played a prominent role in the tree-planting festivities, marching to Eden Park to place soil around trees which had already been set in place. This celebration established a new pattern which provided for schoolchildren the opportunity to create useful memorial groves and be educated to the need of conserving the nation's resources in timber, soil, and wildlife.

Thereafter, at its meeting in St. Paul in 1883, the American Forestry Congress passed a resolution recommending the observance of Arbor Day in the schools of every state; and in 1885 the National Education Association adopted the following resolution:

> *That in view of the valuable results of Arbor Day . . . in the six states where such a day has been observed, alike upon the school and the home, this association recommends the general observance of Arbor Day for schools in all our states.*

Arbor Day spread rapidly throughout the nation and even beyond its borders. By the end of the century, every state and territory of the United States, with only two or three exceptions, observed the celebration. Canada set aside a special day for planting trees and flowers; Spain adopted a similar program; Hawaii established its tree-planting festival, and soon the concept of Arbor Day was adopted throughout the other dependencies of the United States, to England and much of the British Empire, to France, Norway, Russia, Japan, and China.

Currently, Arbor Day celebrations occur on different days in the various states. Thus there is no traditional date for

Arbor Day; rather, tree planting in America has become a massive and continuous conservation endeavor conducted by both individuals and governmental agencies. But each year the President plants a tree at the White House for posterity. The past sixteen Presidents have planted elms, scarlet oaks, Japanese maples, white birches, black walnuts, and magnolias. It might be said that these trees, and all others sown on an Arbor Day, have been planted to bear promise for the future.

LOYALTY DAY

(May 1)

JOHN A. SCHUTZ

*Ever on the first of May did magic walk—the legends
   say—*
*Maidens rose at early dawn to find a dew-encrusted
   lawn,*
*And she who humbly bathed her face in dewdrops in the
   magic place,*
*She, they say, need never fear the curse of freckles for a
   year,*
*And, did she add a certain rune—lo! she would wed a
   lover soon! . . .*

This bit of English verse might also have some basis in the rites of the first recorded celebrants of May 1, the ancient Romans, who undoubtedly passed along the choice of a date for the welcoming spring fete to the conquered Britons.

By the Middle Ages, all England went "a-Maying," gathering flowers and heaping them around and about a beribboned Maypole. It was a day for lightheartedness and laughter.

But this was too much merriment for the prim Puritan colonists, who went so far as to chop down a Maypole erected at Merry Mount Plantation, in Massachusetts, in 1627.

Some remnants of May Day managed to survive the Puritans' displeasure, but it was dealt an almost critical blow by the 1889 international meeting of Socialists which threw out all the flowers and frivolity and renamed it "Labor Day."

Thereafter, May 1 was marked intermittently by militant parades, inflamed addresses, and occasional bombs in almost all of the world's industrialized countries.

But it was the Russian Communists who succeeded in capturing the eyes of the world on May 1. Starting in the 1920's, their parades grew longer and stronger and more military in makeup, finally reaching today's threatening displays of war power and weaponry.

Early in the 1930's, concerned by this apparent disregard for freedom in the face of communism's challenge, units of the Veterans of Foreign Wars began sponsoring celebrations that would properly awaken a spirit of patriotism. They felt the need for a "Loyalty Day" and sought to celebrate it on May 1. The date was deliberately chosen to conflict with the noise and bluster in Moscow.

War veterans from their posts in hundreds of towns across the land organized local parades and festivities. They were frequently hard pressed to define "loyalty" and to devise appropriate ceremonies, but they worked hard and, through correspondence and speakers' bureaus, gained the support of other patriotic organizations. They sent their members to schools, fraternal societies, labor unions, and churches, indeed everywhere, urging people to come forth on May 1 with inspiring programs demonstrating loyalty to America. Thousands of clubs put on special programs, sponsored high-school oratory contests, patriotic plays, and tours to national shrines.

By 1949, forty-nine state and territorial governors had proclaimed May 1 as Loyalty Day. Yet Senator Karl Mundt of North Dakota felt that these local and regional celebrations, although wonderful expressions of patriotism, somehow did not meet the need—"the time has come when freedom has to fight back and when champions of freedom everywhere must stand up and be counted." A *national* day of dedication to loyalty, he said, was appropriate.

His advice was accepted and acted upon by Representative James E. Van Zandt of Pennsylvania. Van Zandt began a campaign in 1950 that was to keep the idea of a national loyalty day constantly before Congress until July 18, 1958, when his efforts were finally rewarded with the passage of Public Law 85-529, making Loyalty Day official. It was to be, said Van Zandt and his colleagues, "a special day for the reaffirmation of loyalty to the United States of America and for the recognition of the heritage of American freedom."

To put into words the feelings, sentiments, and sacrifices of Americans who have lived on this continent over three hundred and fifty years is truly a difficult task, but Loyalty Day orators have attempted to find them. In searching history for these words, they find Ralph Waldo Emerson, the essayist of Concord, who wrote of his belief that Americans had been given a mission "to liberate, to abolish kingcraft, priestcraft, caste, monopoly, to pull down the gallows, to burn up the bloody statute-book, to take in the immigrant, to open the doors of the sea and the fields of the earth. . . ."

They also find James Russell Lowell, who expressed his feelings of loyalty during the crisis of the Civil War: "I love my Country so as only they/Who love a mother fit to die for may . . ."

The words are there to be found, and so are the deeds—the Revolutionary War, the westward expansion, the freeing of the slaves—which inspire them. Loyalty is wrapped up in history, and history in the emotions of the people. Its foundations include pride in our land, its vast spread across a continent, its mighty rivers, luxuriant plains, and lonely prairies.

Loyalty Day, in short, calls upon the nation to recall and revere its past, to put new life into the American spirit, new hope in a bright tomorrow, and new effort to make that tomorrow bright.

CINCO DE MAYO

(May 5)

ROLLIE E. POPPINO

In MUCH OF California, and in the southwestern part of the United States which once belonged to Mexico, the Fifth of May, *Cinco de Mayo,* is a day for honoring the close and friendly relations between the two countries. Many communities hold elaborate ceremonies; there are serious religious services and formal speeches; and there are parades, costumed riders on palomino horses, gay music, feasting, and dancing. The festivities often last all night. It is a happy occasion, when American citizens of Mexican ancestry express pride in their Mexican heritage.

Cinco de Mayo commemorates the victory of the Mexican army over a French invasion force at the city of Puebla on May 5, 1862. Among the national holidays of Mexico, it ranks second only to Independence Day (September 16). For Mexicans, it calls to mind such famous figures as Benito Juárez, the Zapotec Indian who became president and served for many years as the symbol of Mexican independence; Porfirio Díaz, the dashing guerrilla general at Puebla who later was the most powerful dictator the nation has known; Napoleon III of France, who tried to convert Mexico into a French protectorate; and the ill-starred Maximilian, Archduke of Austria, who vainly attempted to rule as emperor of Mexico.

The Battle of Puebla took place during the French intervention in Mexico, which followed immediately after the period of political change and violence known in Mexican history as *La Reforma* (The Reform). *La Reforma* began in 1855 when the Liberal Party came to power after more than twenty years of Conservative administrations.

The Liberals, advocating a system of government similar to that in the United States, set out to destroy the traditional order in which large landholders, the established Church, and the army occupied a privileged position. In a series of sweeping decree-laws, which were consolidated into the Constitution of 1857, special privileges were abolished and the Church was ordered to sell all of its properties not actually used for religious purposes.

The changes were much too drastic to be accepted by the Conservatives and the immediate result was the devastating War of the Reform that wracked Mexico for three years, as rival Liberal and Conservative regimes fought for control of the country. The Conservatives were finally defeated, but the civil war had been costly in lives and property. The economic resources of the Church had been exhausted; both regimes had incurred heavy foreign debts; and the agricultural and mining production on which the national economy depended had been forced to a standstill.

President Juárez resumed leadership of an economically prostrate republic in 1861. The people of Mexico were weary of war but still bitterly divided in their political views.

With their defeat in the War of the Reform, the Conservatives despaired, for there seemed to be no chance to regain power by their own means. The only hope for stability and respect for tradition appeared to lie in the establishment of a monarchy under a foreign prince. In these circumstances, the Conservative leadership looked abroad for advice and assistance, particularly to France, which was then the strongest monarchy in Europe under Emperor Napoleon III.

Napoleon III, eager to equal or surpass the military glories of the first Napoleon, was particularly attracted by the situation in Mexico. Conservative exiles in Paris assured him that

61

French forces would be welcomed with open arms by the Mexican people, who would accept any European prince he might nominate to take the throne of Mexico. His army, reputed to be the finest in Europe, was certainly far superior in training, leadership, and experience to any force that the Juárez regime could muster. Moreover, the outbreak of civil war in the United States in April, 1861, eliminated the likelihood of significant opposition from Washington. The only thing that was needed was an excuse to invade Mexican soil.

That excuse was provided by the Juárez government, which in July, 1861, declared a two-year suspension of payments on Mexico's large foreign debt. The chief creditors— Great Britain, France, and Spain—protested to Juárez, but to no avail. According to international law and custom of the time, the situation called for the use of armed force by the creditor nations. In October, the three powers signed the Convention of London, whereby they agreed to a joint military intervention in Mexico to enforce their claims. In December, a Spanish expedition seized Veracruz, Mexico's major port and the gateway to the capital. The Spaniards were joined by French and British forces in January, 1862. It soon became obvious that France was using the situation as a pretext to gain control of the entire country. Consequently, Great Britain and Spain withdrew from the venture in April, leaving the French forces alone to carry out the occupation of Mexico.

On April 19, the French expedition set out to capture Mexico City, 400 miles inland. Six thousand seasoned troops led by the Comte de Lorencez, an experienced combat general, followed the same invasion route over the lofty Sierra Madres that had been used in 1519 by Hernán Cortés, and later in 1847 by General Winfield Scott, during the war between Mexico and the United States. Lorencez followed the retreating Mexican Army of the East, which kept his column under constant observation and occasional harassing fire while avoiding a direct encounter. On May 4, 1862, the

French camped in sight of Puebla on the plateau approximately halfway between the coast and Mexico City.

The Mexican army, under General Ignacio Zaragoza, decided to make its stand at Puebla. The site offered an excellent defensive position. Two adjoining hills overlooking the city and the road by which the French would enter were partially fortified. Zaragoza occupied the city on the night of May 3, 1862, with a force of five brigades of about one thousand men each. During the following day he deployed the bulk of his troops on the hills and outside the eastern gate, leaving one brigade as a reserve to defend the heart of the city. Neither Zaragoza nor his officers expected to defeat the superbly equipped French column. They hoped to cripple it and slow its advance in order to give Juárez time to rally men for the defense of the capital.

This was as much as they could reasonably expect. Their troops were armed with muskets that had been captured by the British at Waterloo and sold to the Mexican government thirty-five years before. Their artillery was of roughly the same vintage. One brigade was made up largely of recruits who had been in uniform less than three months, and many of the remaining troops were essentially guerrilla fighters, ill-prepared to withstand a mass infantry charge by professional soldiers.

Late in the morning of May 5, 1862, Lorencez attacked. Dividing his men into three groups, he directed two against the hills and sent the third to dislodge Díaz from the entrance to the city. Twice the French stormed up the hills in the face of withering musketry and cannon fire. Both times they reached the top only to be driven back in disorder. As they were retreating after the second charge, a sudden downpour made the steep hillside too muddy for further attack. Cheered by this turn of events, the Mexicans rallied and drove the French in routs toward their camp on the plain below. Meanwhile, the third group of French had been repulsed by a simultaneous attack against its front and both flanks. Holding their fire until they were at point-blank range, Díaz' troops shattered the French column, forcing it into headlong retreat.

The battle lasted about four hours. The Mexicans suffered approximately 250 casualties, while the French lost nearly 1,000 men. The French also lost much of their disdain for the poorly trained and poorly armed Mexican troops. Following his stunning defeat, Lorencez withdrew to the coast to await substantial reinforcements. The intervention continued, but French troops did not move inland again for almost a year. By then they numbered 30,000 men. Napoleon III was obliged to admit that the occupation of Mexico was a far costlier affair than he had anticipated.

Cinco de Mayo immediately entered Mexican annals as a day of glory for national arms. In the dark years that followed, after the French had taken the capital, installed Maximilian as emperor, and driven Juárez and his cabinet to the border of Texas, Mexicans loyal to the republic could take pride in their victory at Puebla over a crack European army. And when Napoleon III withdrew his troops in 1867, the memory of the victory contributed to the resurgence of Mexican nationalism and the overthrow of Maximilian.

During the years of the French intervention, *Cinco de Mayo* was celebrated as a holiday in the territory under control of the Liberals. When Juárez returned to Mexico City in 1867, it became a truly national holiday celebrated by all Mexican citizens.

The commemoration of this day in the United States is not for Mexican-Americans alone. During the period which this date commemorates, our government strongly supported President Juárez in his resistance to the French occupation. We have many historic ties with Mexico, and on *Cinco de Mayo* it is fitting that all Americans recall our common experiences in struggling to preserve political freedom from foreign powers—and our mutual sense of pride in independence.

ARMED FORCES DAY

(Third Saturday in May)

R. ERNEST DUPUY

ONCE EVERY YEAR—on the third Saturday in May—our armed forces hold "open house" for the neighbors. On Armed Forces Day the guests are the American people, and the peoples of our allies and other friendly nations overseas, wherever United States garrisons exist. The occasion marks an accounting—and a demonstration—of the status, strength, and readiness of our armed defenders to sustain not only our own national security but also the cause of freedom throughout the world.

"Power for Peace" is the slogan of Armed Forces Day. It was established by a proclamation of President Harry S. Truman in 1950, three years after the enactment by Congress of the National Security Act, which placed our Army, Navy, and Air Force Departments under a single Department of Defense. Reestablished each year by a Presidential proclamation, the occasion is neither a legal nor a public holiday. It is, rather, a day for spontaneous recognition of, and meditation on, the debt which the nation owes to its men and women in the services. That is why all American citizens are urged to display the Stars and Stripes over their homes on Armed Forces Day.

On that day many thousands visit Army posts, Air Force bases, Navy yards, and warships in port, where they may see for themselves our uniformed troops and the weapons with which they are armed. Demonstrations, weapons exhibits, and maneuvers are the order of the day. Huge intercontinental ballistic missiles, smaller tactical weapons, complicated electronic devices—all are on display. Wherever air bases exist, swift supersonic jets and great cargo planes roar in the air above the spectators. Naval vessels in port and in the yards "dress ship" for the occasion, and their decks are thronged by visitors. Civic demonstrations in the larger cities —in which patriotic societies and veterans' associations take part—include parades and reviews.

Not only do the Regulars strut their stuff on Armed Forces Day, but civilian components—Reserve, National Guard, and Air National Guard—also throw open their armories and other installations, to demonstrate their readiness to meet aggression.

The festivities are not confined to Saturday alone; frequently they spread over the entire weekend, to afford the general public full opportunity to visit all of the various military installations in their respective neighborhoods.

Armed Forces Day represents no specific anniversary. In fact, the date was deliberately chosen as the period least likely to interfere with legal and public holidays already in existence. However, there is nothing artificial about the significance of the day. It represents a combination of the spirit, effort, and goodwill which was publicly demonstrated by the various services on five separate occasions every year: Army Day, Navy Day, Air Force Day, and the anniversaries of the establishment of the Marine Corps and of the Coast Guard.

When we examine each of these days, and their respective meanings, we can realize that Armed Forces Day represents, in capsule form, the proud essence of each service; its history and its specific participation—past and present—in our national military establishment. Over all the panoply of the nuclear age, of mechanization, of the wonders of electronics, a civilian spectator, viewing the battle-streamers on the colors and standards of the various units, can readily see that these soldiers, sailors, and airmen of today carry on the tradition and the patriotic devotion of their forebears, demonstrated in a thousand battles on land, on sea, and in the air since our nation was born in the Revolutionary War.

Navy Day, October 27, represented a double anniversary. Primarily, it commemorated the founding of our Navy on October 27, 1775, when a Committee of the Continental Congress recommended that merchant ships be purchased and converted into war vessels to fight the British navy during the Revolution. Almost equally important was the fact that October 27 was also the birthday of President Theodore Roosevelt, a most ardent admirer and supporter of the Navy. While he was Assistant Secretary of the Navy, just prior to the Spanish-American War, Roosevelt contributed greatly to the Navy's readiness for action. And when the war broke out, his cabled instructions to Commodore (later Admiral) George Dewey, who commanded the Pacific Squadron, led to the Battle of Manila Bay and the destruction of the Spanish fleet in that harbor. The Navy League, an association of civilians who foster the Navy's interests, suggested in 1922 that Navy Day be established, and that same year it was formally instituted by proclamation of President Warren G. Harding.

Army Day came into existence in 1928, through the efforts of the Military Order of the World Wars, a patriotic association of officer-veterans of World War I. Originally celebrated on May 1, as a counter to Communist celebrations held on that date, it was changed to April 6 by a concurrent resolution of the Congress on March 16, 1937. It was on that date in 1917 that the United States declared war against Germany, to "make the world safe for democracy," as President Woodrow Wilson had stated at that time.

Air Force Day is of much later origin. American military aviation was originally part of the Army, beginning on August 1, 1907, when the Aeronautical Division of the Signal Corps was established, until September 18, 1947, when the

Department of Air was established by the same act which instituted the Defense Department. In 1949, the Air Force Association stimulated a movement for a separate commemorative day and September 18—birthday of the independent Air Force—was chosen. Later the commemoration was changed to the second Saturday in September. The date appears to have no specific significance.

The Marine Corps, which was established on November 10, 1775, has for many years celebrated that anniversary by appropriate ceremonies. The Coast Guard, founded on August 4, 1790, as the Revenue Cutter Service, also has honored its birthday with reverence and ceremony for many years. Since the Coast Guard is an element of the Treasury Department in time of peace, but automatically falls under Navy control in wartime—and has participated in all our wars since its inception—it has always taken part in Navy Day celebrations in the past.

The earliest of the service birthdays was that of the Army: June 14, which appropriately enough is also celebrated as Flag Day. It was on June 14, 1775, that the Continental Congress authorized the raising of ten companies of riflemen, who became the nucleus about which the Continental Army was built.

The introduction of Armed Forces Day has in no way diminished the reverence with which the services respect their own individual anniversaries. However, these days now have become intramural, and the individual services render honor to their birthdays with appropriate ceremonies and celebration. But public recognition is reserved for Armed Forces Day—symbolizing the integration of American land, sea, and air power, whose combined effort as a team is essential to provide adequate security for our nation in peace or war.

MEMORIAL DAY

(*May 30*)

CHARLES B. MACDONALD

MANY OF THE MEN in the town had tried to persuade their ladies not to go through with the plan. Memories of the devastating war which had ended only a year before still were too bitter, emotions still too inflamed. Union soldiers, the men feared, might object; and riot and bloodshed might follow.

The women, for their part, would not listen. Not even the most hardened Union soldier, they believed, could object to the compassionate act of decorating the graves of dead men with flowers, particularly when impartiality featured the act. Confederate and Union dead alike, the women reasoned, had died nobly for causes they believed to be right.

Led by a local minister who had been a chaplain in the Confederate army, the women of Columbus, Mississippi, marched, on April 25, 1866, flowers in hand, to Friendship Cemetery, an eighteen-acre tract on the outskirts of the town. There they honored the dead of both sides, men who had fallen not many miles away in the Battle of Shiloh. As the women had predicted, the Union soldiers who occupied the town made no move to interfere.

A brief paragraph describing the event later appeared in a New York newspaper, *The Tribune*. "The women of Columbus," the dispatch noted, "have shown themselves impartial in their offerings made to the memory of the dead.

69

They strewed flowers alike on the graves of the Confederate and of the National soldiers."

One who read that brief account was a young lawyer, Francis Miles Finch, a man who later would attain renown as a jurist and as a co-founder of Cornell University. Reflecting on the event, acutely conscious of the hatred and suspicion that still permeated a nation so recently divided by war, Mr. Finch wrote:

> *By the flow of the inland river*
> *Whence the fleets of iron have fled,*
> *Where the blades of the grave grass quiver,*
> *Asleep are the ranks of the dead:*
> *Under the sod and the dew,*
> *Waiting the judgment-day;*
> *Under the one, the Blue,*
> *Under the other, the Gray.*
>
> . . .
>
> *From the silence of sorrowful hours*
> *The desolate mourners go,*
> *Lovingly laden with flowers*
> *Alike for the friend and the foe:*
> *Under the sod and the dew,*
> *Waiting the judgment-day;*
> *Under the roses, the Blue,*
> *Under the lilies, the Gray.*

Unabashedly sentimental, the poem "The Blue and the Gray" answered a yearning for reconciliation that beat in the hearts of many in the divided nation. Although the ladies of Columbus had not been the first to decorate graves of the dead with flowers—the citizens of Boalsburg, Pennsylvania, had apparently held a somewhat similar ceremony in the summer or fall of 1864—the Columbus event attracted such widespread interest that it is generally considered to have been the initiation of what we now celebrate in the United States as Memorial Day.

It was two years later when a former Union soldier from Ohio wrote to the adjutant-general of the Grand Army of the Republic, an organization of Union veterans, suggesting that the organization might institute an annual practice of honoring the dead of the Civil War with ceremonies and the decorating of graves. Although we do not know his name, this soldier was of German origin and may never have heard of the earlier ceremony in Mississippi; he may have thought instead of patterning the memorial after *Heldengedenktag* (Heroes' Memory Day), long celebrated in Germany each year on March 12.

In any event, on May 5, 1868, local posts of the Grand Army of the Republic were ordered to establish May 30 "for the purpose of strewing with flowers or otherwise decorating the graves of comrades who died in defense of their country during the late rebellion. . . ."

Just why General John A. Logan, commander-in-chief of the Grand Army, chose the thirtieth of May never was specified, but it probably was a natural result of timing that followed the earlier suggestion by the unnamed Union soldier. Certainly it is an appropriate time of the year, for nature's flowers are at their loveliest in late April, May, and early June.

The decoration of graves quickly caught on in the Northern states, while similar commemorations occurred annually throughout the South, but on different days. Celebrations on other dates still take place in some Southern states. April 26, the day when the last major Confederate Army of the East, under General Joseph E. Johnston, surrendered, is commemorated as Memorial Day in four states: Alabama, Georgia, Florida, and Mississippi; on May 10, North and South Carolina celebrate; on May 30, Virginia; and Louisiana and Tennessee choose June 3, birthday of the Confederate president, Jefferson Davis. (In Florida May 30 is a memorial day for veterans of all wars; in Virginia May 30 is Confederate Memorial Day.)

For several years, all commemorations remained unofficial, even though ceremonies at Arlington National Cemetery, just outside the national capital, provided a national focus to the events. The first speaker at Arlington was General James A. Garfield, later to become President of the United States. In subsequent years, the President often has been the principal speaker either at Arlington or at other appropriate places, notably at the battlefield at Gettysburg, Pennsylvania.

Official recognition of Memorial Day as a holiday came in 1873, when New York State designated it a legal holiday. Other states soon followed, and in 1887 the United States Congress made it an official holiday for federal government employees. Next year Congress made it a legal holiday for all persons in the District of Columbia, but to this day there has been no act by Congress establishing Memorial Day on a nationwide basis. This may be because of the origins of the holiday in the violent sectional differences of the Civil War period.

No doubt because of the way it is celebrated, Memorial Day quickly came to be known by many as "Decoration Day." The practice persists, although General Logan and the Grand Army of the Republic insisted that the correct designation was Memorial Day.

Specific methods of celebrating Memorial Day vary throughout the nation, but usually they include military and civic parades and memorial exercises. At installations of the armed forces, flags remain at half-staff until noon, when a ceremony of commemoration for fallen comrades begins. The ceremony almost always includes a twenty-one-gun salute. From ships of the Navy, garlands of flowers are cast upon the sea in memory of those who have died in naval action. Graves of Americans in foreign cemeteries also are decorated. A ceremony at the Tomb of the Unknowns in Arlington Cemetery outside Washington continues to serve as a national focus for the celebration.

As the passing of the years has ameliorated the heartbreak and rancor of the Civil War, Memorial Day gradually has come to mean more than a day on which to commemorate the dead of that war. Like the German *Heldengedenktag,* and like World War I's Armistice Day in Great Britain, France, and Italy, it has become a day for honoring the dead of all the nation's wars. More and more it has also become accepted as a special day for honoring not only those killed in combat but the dead from one's immediate circle of friends and family.

More recently, Memorial Day has taken on a new aspect for many Americans, both because of the closeness of the date to the birthday (May 29) of the youthful, assassinated thirty-fourth President of the United States, John F. Kennedy, and because of the location of the late President's grave on a hillside in Arlington National Cemetery. Certainly the young President's violent death at the hands of an assassin occurred as much in the front ranks of the perpetual battle for human liberty as that of any other soldier, sailor, or airman who preceded him. His death profoundly affected all the American people, and thus may so adequately serve as a kind of symbol of the solemn, somber nature of all that we commemorate on Memorial Day.

FLAG DAY

(*June 14*)

BOYD C. SHAFER

JUNE 14, Flag Day, celebrates the birthday of the American flag. Born of a Joint Resolution of the Continental Congress on June 14, 1777, the flag has become over the years the supreme symbol of the nation, its ideals, its triumphs, its tragedies.

The flag was over one hundred years old before a special celebration was established. In 1893, the mayor of Philadelphia asked for a display of flags on all civic buildings and that schools, too, take note of this anniversary; in 1897, the governor of New York did the same. The idea spread. In 1916, by proclamation, President Woodrow Wilson asked that Flag Day be observed throughout the nation, and, in 1949, Congress officially designated June 14 as Flag Day and requested the President each year to proclaim the anniversary.

"This beloved emblem," President Truman proclaimed in 1949, "which flies above all our people of whatever creed or race, signalizes our respect for human rights and the protection such rights are afforded under our form of government." Behind the emblem are the ideals expressed in the Declaration of Independence and the Preamble to the Constitution that "all men . . . are endowed . . . with certain unalienable rights . . . life, liberty, and the pursuit of happiness," and that in establishing their government the people of the United States desired "to form a more perfect Union, establish Justice, insure domestic Tranquility, provide for the common defense, promote the general Welfare, and secure the Blessings of Liberty . . ."

Since early times people have displayed objects, banners, and flags to indicate allegiance. Probably one of the first true flags, carried by Roman cavalry, was a square piece of fringed cloth hung on a crossbar at the end of a spear. Europeans carried their flags in this manner until the Middle Ages when invading Saracens came with flags attached to the side of a staff. Several modern flags stem from the Crusades when the cross was the symbol used by the Christians. Denmark's national flag, the Dannebrog, a white cross on a red field, is one of the oldest national flags.

At sea, where identification is especially necessary, symbols were first painted on sails, later incorporated into banners hoisted to the top of the mast, and by the sixteenth century modern usages were established. On land, flag masts were set up at forts to indicate possession by or the presence of rulers. Many modern flags have been patterned after the tricolor of the French Revolution, a flag which became the symbol of a nation of citizens rather than of the ruler. Serving first as simple identification, flags have become emblems of many groups and institutions, of nations, and of international organizations such as the Red Cross and the United Nations.

Before the authorized national flag of 1777, the American colonists fought under several flags. At Bunker Hill, according to the artist John Trumbull, who was there but was not always an accurate witness, Colonial soldiers displayed a red flag with a green pine tree on a white field with the words: "An Appeal to God," and also a solid red flag. The first authorized fleet sailed out of Massachusetts early in January, 1776, under a flag similar to the green pine-tree one, adding a coiled rattlesnake below the pine tree and the words: "Don't Tread on Me." When the Continental Army under Washington came formally into existence on January 1, 1776, a ceremony was staged on Prospect Hill, Cambridge,

Massachusetts, in which a new flag was hoisted on a seventy-six-foot flagstaff. This Great or Grand Union Flag was a simple modification of the Meteor Flag of Great Britain. Six horizontal white stripes were imposed on the large red field making thirteen stripes for the thirteen Colonies. Although obsolete after the Declaration of Independence, the Grand Union Flag was the first national flag and from it, with one simple change, the Stars and Stripes was created.

The Second Continental Congress of the young United States (or Colonies) on June 14, 1777, passed the resolution which established the basic pattern of the flag: "That the flag of the United States be made of thirteen stripes, alternate red and white; that the union be thirteen stars, white in a blue field, representing a new constellation." As Congress did not supply the Army and Navy with flags, Revolutionary War flags varied in detail. Very likely John Paul Jones first flew the new Stars and Stripes at sea, on his sloop the *Ranger*, when he sailed for France in November, 1777, commissioned to convey the news of Burgoyne's surrender. The following February, the French fleet gave the new American flag a nine-gun salute, the first foreign recognition of the Stars and Stripes.

When Vermont and Kentucky entered the Union the flag was changed in 1794 to contain fifteen stars and fifteen stripes. This flag, unchanged for almost a quarter of a century, was the inspiration of the national anthem, "The Star-Spangled Banner." It was also the first flag to span the continent, with the Lewis and Clark expedition of 1804–06.

As new states came into the Union, it was evident that new stripes could not continue to be added. A third act of Congress, April 4, 1818, prescribed thirteen stripes and twenty stars, and provided that a star be added for each state admitted. This law remains the legal basis of the flag, which after twenty-six changes now has fifty stars. President Eisenhower, in 1959, issued an Executive Order (No. 10834) which set official standards. Exact dimensions and proportions are prescribed. Of the thirteen stripes, seven are red, and six stripes run below the union. The stars are five-pointed and alternate six and five in nine rows. Thus the form of the flag, changed many times over the years, finally became fixed.

Many legends about the early flag are unverifiable. The dramatic tale of Betsy Ross, perhaps the most persistent in American folklore, has little historical foundation. That she was a seamstress and was paid for making colors for the Pennsylvania navy in May, 1777, there is proof. Even less verifiable is the story of the quilting party at Portsmouth, on July 4, 1777, at which beautiful young women were said to have made the flag for John Paul Jones from slices of their best silk gowns. Orators and writers have been anxious to ascribe special significance to the colors chosen for the flag. Blue has been said to represent justice; the stars in a circle to symbolize perpetuity of the union; red to signify defiance (or the lifeblood of brave men); and white to stand for purity. Evidence indicates that such sentiments were after-thoughts. Another popular but erroneous idea is that each state is represented by a particular star in the union, arranged according to the order of its ratification of the Constitution. Sometimes, it must also be regretfully stated, individuals and groups have used the flag to adorn a tale or to forward their own private interests.

The story of the national anthem is well recorded although the author himself never wrote down how he composed it. Francis Scott Key, a Washington lawyer detained on a British ship in the Baltimore Harbor, September 13, 1814, watched the British bombard Fort McHenry. When the cannonading ceased late that night he could not tell whether the fort had surrendered. In the dawn's early light the flag was still there and the enemy preparing to depart. Jubilantly Key wrote down notes which he polished into verses in a Baltimore hotel soon afterward. For tune and meter he used an old popular melody, "Anacreon in Heaven." The song was printed as a broadside and on September 20 it appeared in a Baltimore newspaper, the *Patriot*. Gradually "The Star-Spangled

Banner" grew in popularity until, in 1931, Congress designated it the national anthem.

The star-spangled banner which waved over Fort McHenry is still preserved. It was made by Mary Young Pickersgill, whose home in Baltimore is called the Flag House, and her daughter. The Pickersgills, who received $409.90 for their work, used 400 yards of handwoven bunting. The flag is now displayed in its full length at the Smithsonian Institution in Washington, D.C.

About sixty-eight patriotic and civic organizations met in Washington in 1923, under the auspices of the American Legion, to draft a code of flag etiquette. This served as a guide for many years. Finally, in 1942, the rules and customs for the display and use of the flag were codified in Public Law 829 of the 77th Congress. The details of this code can be found in standard encyclopedias. The code declares in substance that at all times the flag is the emblem of the United States and should be viewed and handled with respect. During ceremonies of hoisting or lowering the flag or when it passes in review, individuals present stand at attention and salute. At only a few places may the flag be flown day and night: on the Capitol Building in Washington, for example; at Taos, New Mexico, where Kit Carson nailed a Union flag in 1861; and atop Mount Suribachi, on Iwo Jima in the Pacific, to honor the United States Marines who planted it there in World War II.

The Pledge of Allegiance is incorporated in the same law. First published in the *Youth's Companion* for September 8, 1892, in connection with a school celebration of Columbus Day, it was written by Francis Bellamy and other members of that magazine's staff. Printed then in leaflet form, it was distributed about the country; possibly as many as 12 million children may have taken it. Changed but little from the original, the official wording now is:

I pledge allegiance to the flag of the United States of America and to the Republic for which it stands, one

*nation under God, indivisible, with liberty and justice
for all.*

President Woodrow Wilson, in his speech on Flag Day of
1917, spoke for many Americans when he said:

*This flag which we honor and under which we serve is
the emblem of our unity, our power, our thought and
purpose as a nation. It has no other character than that
which we give it from generation to generation. The
choice is ours. It floats in majestic silence above the
hosts that execute those choices whether in peace or
war. And yet, though silent, it speaks to us . . . of the
men and women who went before us and of the records
they wrote upon it. We celebrate the day of its
birth. . . .*

INDEPENDENCE DAY

(July 4)

RICHARD M. LEIGHTON

"WHY IS IT," asked the man from Mars, "that every year on July 4, you Americans take off from work and spend the day shooting off firecrackers, watching parades, and listening to speeches? Pretty dull speeches, too, I might add."

"I don't know that it's any of your business," the American answered irritably. "I suspect you're only looking for a chance to show off your superior knowledge. You Martians have been watching the earth through telescopes for several thousand years now, and you know as well as I do why we celebrate July 4. Anyway, we don't shoot firecrackers much any more; we have supervised community fireworks at night."

"I think he's making a survey," observed the Frenchman. "Yesterday he was asking me about Bastille Day. He does know what Independence Day is, but he wants to know what you *think* about it. Incidentally, so do I."

"And we," chorused the Englishman and the Pole.

The man from Mars nodded. "For the folks back home," he explained. "My paper is running a series on 'Historic Earthly Holidays.'"

"Well," the American began, "we celebrate July 4 because it's Independence Day. It's the day we won our independence from the British—in 1776. I think."

"Oh, come on, now, Yank," interrupted the Englishman.

"Give us our due. It took you a few more years to do that—until about 1783, as I recall."

"*With* outside help, too," added the Frenchman. "Remember Lafayette?"

"And Kosciusko," said the Pole.

"Well, I guess we didn't *win* independence in 1776." The American looked flustered. "And we certainly did have help." He brightened. "Now I remember. July 4 was the day we *declared* our independence—the Declaration of Independence." He looked around triumphantly.

"Now that's most interesting," said the man from Mars, thumbing through some notes. "I happened to be looking through the telescope about that time, and—ah, yes, here it is—the American Colonies declared their independence from Great Britain on *July 2, 1776*—not July 4. I wrote it down."

There was a long silence. Then a new voice broke in. "Actually you're both right."

Everyone turned, startled. "Who are you?" demanded the man from Mars.

The newcomer coughed apologetically. "I am a Professor of History. I hope you don't mind my butting in. It's true, you know—both of you are right. Though I'm afraid that my young friend here," he turned and looked kindly at the American, "is less certain of his facts than you are."

"I am quite certain of mine, I assure you," said the man from Mars stiffly. "Our telescopes do not lie. If I am right, how can he be right, too?"

The Professor of History smiled reassuringly. "If you will all indulge me, I shall be happy to explain. Now, then. Let us try to picture the situation as it appeared back in June and early July of 1776 to some fifty provincial gentlemen meeting in a borrowed first-floor room of the Old State House —now Independence Hall—in Philadelphia. You may visit that room today; it looks very much now as it did then.

"These gentlemen were the Second Continental Congress of the thirteen seaboard colonies of British North America south of Canada. History calls them the 'founding fathers'

81

of our nation. Actually, most of them were fairly young, but they were gentlemen of substance, leaders of their communities, and known throughout the Colonies—aristocratic planters like Tom Jefferson of Virginia; well-to-do merchants like John Hancock; lawyers and politicians like John Adams; and seventy-year-old Ben Franklin of Philadelphia who had an international reputation as a scientist and diplomat.

"The Congress had already been in session for more than a year, since shortly after the outbreak of fighting with the British in the spring of 1775. Surely you all remember Paul Revere's ride and the Battles of Lexington, Concord, and all that. At first there had been little thought of separation from Great Britain. Like their predecessors in the First Continental Congress in 1774, these men had begun by protesting their loyalty to the British Crown and by seeking a basis for reconciliation. But they insisted on their rights as free Englishmen, which they said had been violated—through taxation and economic restrictions—by the British Parliament in which they were not represented.

"As the months passed, the rush of events pushed old grievances back into history, and hope of reconciliation grew dim. Soon the Continental Congress took steps which constituted a kind of commitment to seek independence— opening American ports to foreign trade, in defiance of the old imperial restrictions, organizing revolutionary provincial governments, appealing to France for aid. The real test, as the delegates in Philadelphia well knew, lay ahead. An American invasion of Canada had ended in disaster, and British forces stiffened by German mercenary troops were mustering to attack New York. The future looked grim, indeed.

"During May and June, the Congress wrestled with its conscience and its fears. The moderates hoped the King's commissioners might yet bring offers of an honorable reconciliation, while the radicals pressed for an immediate break. On June 7, the moderates gained a three-week postponement of debate on a resolution for independence submitted by Richard Henry Lee of Virginia, but on July 2 the resolution was finally brought to a vote and passed unanimously. The resolution declared that 'these United Colonies are, and of right ought to be, free and independent States; that they are absolved from all allegiance to the British Crown, and that all political connection between them and the State of Great Britain is, and ought to be, totally dissolved.'

"With that vote, gentlemen," the Professor stated, "the thirteen Colonies finally and irrevocably broke their ties with Great Britain. The resolution of July 2 was the original, and, I suppose one might say, the *real* 'declaration of independence.' In that sense, sir"—he addressed the man from Mars —"you are right."

"But, Professor," blurted the American, "you said . . ."

"Patience, my young friend. There is more. Immediately after the vote on the Lee resolution, the Congress proceeded to the next item on the agenda, a draft 'Declaration by the Representatives of the United States of America, in General Congress assembled.' This soon-to-be-famous document had been submitted by a committee appointed early in June when the Lee resolution was first brought up. The committee had been instructed, in anticipation of the vote on the resolution, to draft a pronouncement that would, in effect, *proclaim to the world the reasons for declaring independence.* The chairman of the committee, and author of the declaration, was, as you probably know, thirty-three-year-old Tom Jefferson.

"The Congress worked over Jefferson's draft with a fine-tooth comb. They made relatively few substantive changes but, for political reasons, excised something like a quarter of his choicest phrases. Poor Jefferson suffered through the ordeal in silence.

"On July 4, the job was finished and the Declaration of Independence, as we call it, was approved. Despite the editing—or because of it—the declaration is a beautiful and stirring document, gentlemen, from its opening phrases: 'When, in the course of human events, it becomes necessary for one people to dissolve the political bands which have connected them with another . . .' to its final, cadenced

'. . . we mutually pledge to each other our lives, our fortunes, and our sacred honor.'

"So you see, gentlemen, the Congress did, as my young friend stated, 'declare independence' on July 4, even though it had already done so on July 2. This is literally true, despite the explanatory purpose of the second declaration, since the Congress incorporated the July 2 resolution bodily in the final paragraph of Jefferson's paper—by which time, doubtless, he was too numb to care."

The man from Mars looked annoyed. "It appears to me, Professor, that this is a pure quibble. The whole point of my original observation was that you Americans have obviously been celebrating the wrong date for all these years. The really significant event occurred on July 2; the declaration approved on July 4 was merely a gaudy embellishment, an elegant afterthought. I'll wager the good gentlemen of the Congress did their celebrating on the second, not the fourth."

"No, as a matter of fact," mused the Professor, "they celebrated on July 8 that year. It is one of the minor ironies of our story. However, you have a point. John Adams himself predicted at the time that later generations of Americans would celebrate *July* 2 'as the great anniversary festival.' He felt that it should be commemorated 'by solemn acts of devotion to God Almighty . . . with pomp and parade, with shows, games, sports, guns, bells, bonfires, and illuminations, from one end of this continent to the other, from this time forward forevermore.'"

There was another long silence, broken finally by the Englishman. "Well, Yank, it does look as though you chaps have got your dates a bit mixed, but I suppose it's too late to do anything about it now. I wouldn't fret over it. Water over the dam, and all that sort of thing."

"With us, too," put in the Frenchman, "history has its little joke. In my country we commemorate the fall of the Bastille, an ancient prison in Paris, on July 14, 1789, as symbolizing the triumph of liberty over royal tyranny.

Actually July 14 had already been made an official holiday, for different reasons, two years before."

The Pole spoke slowly and softly. "For America, gentlemen, I see no joke, only a great blessing. You are a fortunate people. A few years after your great Declaration of Independence was written, my own people felt the conqueror's heel—not for the first time, nor the last. History did not choose for you July 4 instead of July 2; you made the choice yourselves, and it was a wise one. What is important here is not the event, but the idea—the great and enduring idea of liberty—and this idea is enshrined for all time in the imperishable words and phrases of Jefferson's noble declaration. Cherish this document, American, and guard well the liberty it symbolizes. One day you may have to fight for it again."

After a moment, the man from Mars coughed and took out his pencil. "If you don't mind," he asked respectfully, "would you repeat that, slowly. I think my editor would like it."

"Amen," said the Professor of History.

V-J DAY

(September 2)

ARMIN RAPPAPORT

AT 9:00 A.M. on September 2, 1945, representatives of the Japanese government, military and civilian, boarded the battleship USS *Missouri*, anchored in Tokyo Harbor, and signed the documents signifying their country's surrender. World War II was officially over, 1,364 days 5 hours 44 minutes after Pearl Harbor.

The ceremony was impressive. General Douglas Mac-Arthur, who had been appointed Supreme Commander for the Allied Powers in Japan, was surrounded by high-ranking officers from all the nations which had fought in the war, as he awaited the Japanese. On one side of him stood General Jonathan M. Wainwright, the American officer who had been forced to surrender at Corregidor early in the war and who had been a prisoner of the Japanese until the end. On the other side of him stood General Arthur Percival, the British commander who had surrendered Singapore.

The American flag which flew from the *Missouri*'s main staff was the same flag which had been flying over the Capitol in Washington on December 7, 1941, at the moment that the Japanese attacked Pearl Harbor. And on one of the *Missouri*'s bulkheads in plain view of the assembled delegates was tacked the flag which Commodore Matthew C. Perry had flown from his ship when he entered Tokyo Bay (then called Yedo Bay) in 1853 to open relations with Japan.

86

This then was the first V-J Day, marking Allied victory over Japan—a victory gained mainly by the armed forces of the United States.

Actually, the war had virtually ended on August 14, when President Harry S. Truman announced from the White House at 7:00 P.M. that he had received a message from the Japanese emperor which stated the decision to surrender. The end had not been unexpected. Atom bombs had been dropped on Hiroshima on August 6 and on Nagasaki on August 9. Since that time, newspapers had been carrying banner headlines suggesting that the effects of the most revolutionary bombs in history would lead to the end of hostilities. Additional pressure was placed on Japan by Russia's entry into the Pacific war on the Ninth.

And so, on America's day of victory, the President at once declared a two-day holiday. Pandemonium broke loose. People wept openly, danced in the streets, and embraced each other. Two million people jammed Times Square in New York City to celebrate the end of the war. Deep emotions, pent up for three years and eight months, were released, for the war had been hard and bitter and the casualties heavy.

Although there had been little doubt after the beginning of 1943 of an ultimate American victory, the fanatical resistance of the Japanese made every advance costly. Before the war was over in the Pacific, 41,322 Americans had died and about 130,000 were wounded. Island by island, the United States land, sea, and air forces had fought their way across the broad Pacific to the Japanese homeland and to victory. American soldiers and airmen had also fought beside their British and Chinese allies to reconquer Burma, and to repulse the final desperate Japanese efforts to defeat and conquer long-suffering China.

The war against Japan had been waged across half of the globe, from the coasts of Ceylon and India in the Indian Ocean to the Pacific shore of the United States, from Alaska to Australia. Since most of this vast region is covered by oceans, the victory had been primarily one of sea power, with the United States Navy—staunchly supported by the naval forces of our British, Australian, New Zealand, and Dutch allies—leading the way. The victory was secured, however, by seizing and holding bases on the great land masses and tiny islands throughout the entire region. Credit for the conquest of these base areas is due as much to the gallantry and heroism of our soldiers, marines, and airmen as it is to our sailors. From these bases, the combined land, sea, and air might of the United States pressed forward relentlessly, until stricken Japan sued for peace.

Since 1945, the anniversary of the signing of the surrender documents has been declared an official holiday. But the day is not usually marked by ceremonies. This is not a day for parades, for grand meetings of veterans, for dinners, or for speeches. Families of servicemen who lost their lives decorate graves in national cemeteries; occasionally small groups of veterans of particular battles or units join together to reminisce. Today Japan is no longer an enemy and, indeed, is much different from the autocratic and militaristic Japan which attacked Pearl Harbor without warning, launching the war in the Pacific. She is now a peaceful nation operating under a democratic constitution, a member of the United Nations, and a staunch ally of the United States in the present worldwide struggle against communism. We and the Japanese, friends who can recall respectfully the fighting qualities of the other, have neither the need nor desire to stir up again the bitterness of the war years.

If there be any formal ceremonies commemorating the end of the war, they may well take the form of repeating the words of General MacArthur which he read immediately after the surrender on the *Missouri*'s deck. "Today the guns are silent. A great tragedy has ended. A great victory has been won. The skies no longer rain death—the seas bear only commerce—men everywhere walk upright in the sunlight. The entire world lies quietly at peace. The Holy Mission has been completed . . . I speak for the thousands of silent

88

lips, forever stilled among the jungles and the beaches and in the deep waters of the Pacific . . . for the unnamed brave millions homeward bound to take up the challenge of that future which they did so much to salvage from the brink of disaster. . . . We must go forward to preserve in peace what we won in war."

LABOR DAY

(First Monday in September)

GRACE P. HAYES

MOST OF US think of Labor Day, the first Monday in September, as marking the end of summer and the beginning of fall. Vacations end; school begins. It is one last day off from work while the weather is still warm and there are things to do outdoors. But behind the pleasure and the parades, the speeches and the swimming, the celebrations and the picnics, Labor Day has a deeper significance.

In 1882, when Peter J. McGuire, a founder of the labor union called the United Brotherhood of Carpenters and Joiners of America, proposed "setting aside one day in the year to be designated as 'Labor Day,' to be established as a general holiday for the laboring classes," the labor movement in the United States had for many years been an important factor in American life. Much had already been done to improve the lot of the workingman.

At the beginning of the nineteenth century, the life of a man who worked in a factory or a mine, and the life of his family, were very different from the life of a working family today. Their children could not go to school; there were few public schools for them to go to. The children of many poor families often had to get up in the early morning and go to work in a factory while it was still dark outside. It was

90

frequently dark inside, too, and dirty—freezing cold in winter and stifling hot in summer.

People worked all day long, the children sometimes doing jobs that were considered too dangerous for adults. At noon there was a little time off for lunch, then back to work again for the rest of the day. At quitting time it was dark again. There was no time for play, and many people rarely saw the sun, for they worked six or even seven days a week. If a worker got sick, no one cared except his family, and when he got well there was often no job to go back to. Pay was very poor, and because there were always plenty of other workers to take a job, a person who asked for more pay was likely to be fired.

Gradually, some of the workers decided to act together to try to improve the conditions under which they worked. Those in one factory or industry, or in one craft, such as plumbing or carpentering, began to form unions. Union leaders went to the men who employed them, demanding reforms such as shorter working hours, higher pay, or better social conditions. They also went into politics to try to get free schooling for their children and to secure other social reforms for laboring people.

Sometimes employers granted requests from the unions or worked out a compromise, but frequently they refused. Then the workers might strike, stopping work entirely until a settlement was reached. Some strikes were very effective; but when employers refused to yield, or retaliated by refusing to permit the workers to return to their jobs, or hired nonunion workers to take their places, strikes continued for weeks or even months and sometimes erupted in violence.

During the 1830's many unions were formed. They managed to win some improvements for their industries and to make people aware of the needs and rights of workingmen. A great stride was taken in 1840 when President Martin Van Buren ordered a ten-hour working day on all government projects, with no reduction in wages. About the same time some unions also succeeded in getting ten- or

91

eleven-hour days on nongovernment jobs. In more and more states, unions helped to obtain free public schools for all children. But it was after the Civil War, when business and industry were expanding rapidly, that the labor movement really began to grow.

In 1869, Uriah S. Stephens, a tailor from Philadelphia, founded a union that was open to all workers. Called the Noble Order of the Knights of Labor, it started as a secret organization, with secret passwords and special rituals. Among other things, it favored an eight-hour working day and equal pay for equal work by women.

It was when the Knights of Labor was strongest that Mr. McGuire proposed a holiday for labor. As he himself wrote later:

> . . . *There were other worthy holidays representative of the religious, civil, and military spirit, but none representative of the industrial spirit—the great vital force of every nation. [I] suggested the first Monday in September of every year for such a holiday, as it would come at the most pleasant season of the year, nearly midway between the Fourth of July and Thanksgiving, and would fill a wide gap in the chronology of legal holidays.*

The Central Labor Union of New York City adopted his suggestion and, on September 5, 1882, sponsored the first Labor Day parade and festival. Many of the marchers carried signs urging improvement in working conditions in their industries. Others asked for an eight-hour day. The celebration was a big success, and dramatized the importance of labor.

The idea of a special holiday to honor workers grew. In 1893, with thirty-six states already celebrating official Labor Days at various times during the year, the United States Congress began to consider legislation to establish a national holiday. "By making each year a public holiday for the benefit of workingmen," said the Labor Committee of the House of Representatives, "the equality and dignity of labor is emphasized."

The congressional bill to make the first Monday of September a national Labor Day was signed into law by President Cleveland on June 28, 1894.

By this time a new labor organization had appeared on the scene. Increasingly, workers had grown to prefer unions devoted to their own crafts rather than the all-inclusive Knights of Labor. In 1886, a federation was formed of craft unions, in which the strongest were the carpenters, cigar makers, printers, iron- and steelworkers, and iron molders. This was the American Federation of Labor (AFL), which flourished under the leadership of Samuel Gompers. Originally a cigar maker by trade, Gompers had been interested in the problems of workers since he started to work in a cigar factory at the age of thirteen. The American Federation of Labor grew rapidly, and due to its efforts, both the well-being and the prestige of the worker increased. In the 1930's another federation was formed, with the objective of organizing unions of all the workers in such big new industries as the manufacture of automobiles. The Congress of Industrial Organizations (CIO), as this federation was called, joined with the AFL in 1955 to form the AFL-CIO, America's principal national labor organization.

Strikes have continued to be labor's chief weapon, and there have been many long and tragic ones during the past years. In 1892, for example, steelworkers on strike at the Carnegie Steel Company in Homestead, Pennsylvania, engaged in a two-day armed battle with men hired to guard the plant, and several men were killed or wounded. In 1894, President Cleveland sent federal troops to intervene in the strike of the American Railway Union against the Pullman Company in Chicago. Long strikes, with no pay coming in for food, rent, or clothing, caused serious hardship to workers and their families. So the unions built up funds to provide food and other necessities for striking workers.

Increasingly, however, employers and workers alike have realized the desirability of trying to settle their differences without resort to strikes, and the principle of collective bargaining has been accepted. In collective bargaining, representatives of the employers sit down at a table with union leaders who represent the workers. Labor's basic demands have more often been met by employers who now generally realize that it is to their advantage that their workers be contented and prosperous; and labor leaders, for their part, instead of pursuing revolutionary aims as some had strongly advocated, have tended to adopt as their objectives, higher wages and better working conditions, and to realize, moreover, that only a prosperous business can afford to pay generous salaries.

The United States is not unique in celebrating a Labor Day. Many nations celebrate it on the first day of May. But more often than not theirs is a holiday for workers alone and a different sort of holiday entirely, for in some cases they do not think as we do about labor and laboring people. In countries where people are divided into classes according to the work that they do or their family heritage, the man who works with his hands—the plumber, the bricklayer, the factory worker, the carpenter—is at the bottom of the list. He is not considered to be as good as an office worker, a doctor, a lawyer, a businessman, or a very wealthy person who does not work at all. In many countries it is even considered a disgrace to dirty one's hands at work.

In our country, however, work is respected. Our foremost citizens, Presidents among them, are proud to say that they have earned a living by working with their hands. And no one is denied privileges that others enjoy because of the kind of work that he does.

In many nations, Labor Day is a holiday for workers to protest labor conditions, social conditions, or politics. In the United States it is a holiday for everybody, and all factories and most businesses close. Government officials, clergymen, and prominent citizens of all kinds—as well as labor leaders

—make speeches about the importance and the dignity of labor. Labor Day has become a day to pause and rest, a day to renew our conviction that the work of each of us, whatever it may be, is a contribution to the greatness of our nation.

CITIZENSHIP DAY

(September 17)

GAY M. HAMMERMAN

ALL AMERICANS are here because someone migrated. Even the Indians, scientists now believe, came to America from somewhere else, probably Asia, in search of a better life. Except for the Indians, who probably made most of the journey by land, each migrant crossed a great ocean in traveling from his old life to his new life. English Pilgrims, African Negroes, Germans, Italians, Greeks, Chinese, and many, many others—each made the long voyage on a crowded, wave-tossed ship. Somewhere in the ancestry of almost every American is the misery of seasickness and the danger of death by violence, drowning, suffocation, or disease. And in that ancestry is also a driving love of freedom.

Every year more than 100,000 new Americans, born in other countries, become citizens. Every year, also, almost 3,000,000 young Americans, descendants of immigrants, become old enough to claim one of the most important aspects of American citizenship—the right to vote. September 17, the anniversary of the signing of the Constitution, is called Citizenship Day, a special day to honor these new citizens. It also honors the Constitution that guarantees to all of us the government and rights for which so many have crossed the oceans. Many new Americans take their oath of allegiance and become naturalized citizens on Citizenship Day. For most of them naturalization is a moving experience, the climax of years of effort. Tears are shed, and special celebrations follow.

By 1787, when the Constitution was written, immigrants had been coming from Europe for almost two hundred years. Among the Constitution writers were men who had migrated from England, Scotland, Ireland, and the British West Indies. The sufferings of all the immigrants, from the earliest settlers to the settlers of the early twentieth century, were remarkably similar. The Pilgrims were cheated and robbed during their long, roundabout voyage; they were imprisoned, separated from their families; they were often sick, cold, and hungry in their search for a land where they could live and pray as they wished. The Negroes suffered the most of any immigrants, brought as slaves against their will, in chains, with their past traditions brutally taken from them, and with little hope that they would ever stop being possessions of other people. The ocean passage was also cruel for many others. In 1870, of 544 immigrants on one ship from Germany, 108 died in their filthy, crowded quarters, where they had little food and no doctor.

Three great waves of immigration in the nineteenth and twentieth centuries brought far more immigrants than had come in all the earlier years. The first wave was in the 1840's and 1850's. Most of the people it brought were Irish, German, or English. Many of the Irish were fleeing the starvation of the great potato famine of 1846–48; some of the Germans had left their old country because of the failure of a democratic revolution there. A British observer wrote of these Germans, ". . . the young, the restless, and the imaginative thirst for their ideal freedom." They hoped to find it in America. In the British Isles, the same thirst for freedom was felt by many who left. The American labor leader Samuel Gompers was in part inspired to come here by a song. So was the father of the leading American industrialist Andrew Carnegie. The song went:

97

To the West! to the West! to the land of the free
Where the mighty Missouri rolls down to the sea;
Where a man is a man if he's willing to toil,
And the humblest may gather the fruits of the soil.

* * *

Away! far away, let us hope for the best
And build up a home in the land of the West.

The second, and greater, wave of immigrants reached its peak in 1882, bringing mostly Germans, Scandinavians, and Englishmen, though many were now coming from southern Europe and from China. Then, between 1900 and 1914, came the greatest wave of all, reaching its peak in 1907, when almost a million and a half people came, mostly from southern and eastern Europe—Italy, Poland, Russia, Greece, and Turkey. Many were also from Japan. Some immigrants of the 1880's helped open the farmlands of the West; others built railroads across the country. Those of the early twentieth century built skyscrapers and dug subways.

As the new Americans and their children became more at home in America, they became doctors, lawyers, businessmen, teachers, and scientists. Most of them kept enough of their old-country customs to add rich variety to their new country—meals with new spice, music with different melodies. Many brought special skills in woodcarving, stonecutting, needlecraft. Many came from simple societies in which family strength and unity were especially important, and they maintained this tradition in America. Some groups, including the Chinese and the Jews from eastern Europe, brought a traditional devotion to learning that raised the standards of other Americans. Many new Americans, including the Negroes who were rising slowly toward full citizenship during the period of the great migrations, came from cultures that allowed a freer expression and understanding of human emotion than had earlier American traditions. This liberating influence shows itself in American music, writing, theater, dance, painting—in every aspect of our life.

98

Religion was the one thing that almost no immigrant would give up in his new world. Before the great migration, the United States was a predominantly Protestant nation with little islands of other worshipers; the immigrants made it a varied society in which, although religion is given high value, there is no one typical American religion.

The third and last great wave of immigrants was stopped by World War I. After 1924, under new United States laws, only about 150,000 people could enter each year, and the numbers from each country were also limited. There was less land and less need for workers than there had been earlier. And, surprisingly, many people were also afraid that having too many immigrants would change the country for the worse. People still came in search of freedom and a better life; some were refugees from Nazi Germany in the 1930's and Communist Hungary in 1956. But the great migrations had ended. The many Puerto Ricans who came during the 1950's to the United States mainland, and especially to New York City, were already citizens when they arrived. They remind other citizens that not all Americans speak English or live in the continental United States.

Because Citizenship Day is celebrated on the anniversary of the signing of the Constitution, it reminds each American of his duty as a citizen to support this document. No other written constitution has lasted so long in modern times. It gives us a national government that is strong and effective, and at the same time respects and protects the basic rights of all people. Citizenship Day brings old and new Americans together in their common immigrant background and their common joy in United States citizenship.

AMERICAN INDIAN DAY

(Fourth Friday in September in most states)

RALPH K. ANDRIST

THE FIRST CITIZENS of this continent waited a long time before a holiday was dedicated to them. It is still not a perfect tribute because American Indian Day is not observed in all states, and those that celebrate it are not in complete agreement on a choice of date.

In 1914, a Blackfoot Indian, Red Fox James, rode more than 4,000 miles on horseback, calling on state governors and other influential people to argue that there should be an annual Indian Day. His reception was almost always favorable, and in December he went on to Washington to give to the White House the endorsements which he had received. The idea probably would have stopped there if it had not been taken up by the annual assembly of the American Indian Association which met the next year (1915) in Lawrence, Kansas. Well over a thousand Indians, representing more than a hundred tribes, were present, and after discussing a proposal for an annual American Indian Day, voted their approval. The president of the Association issued a proclamation, which said in part:

> . . . *we do invite every American who loves his country and would uphold its honor and dignity, to celebrate this day and consider our early philosophy, our love of freedom, our social institutions, and our*

100

history in the full light of truth and the balances of jus-
tice, in honest comparison with the annals of other
races, and to draw therefrom these noble things that
we believe are worthy of emulation. . . .

This plea for recognition and justice was made at a time
when most Indians were still denied such basic rights of
American citizenship as the vote. Nevertheless, the idea of
American Indian Day struck a spark; the day was first
generally observed in New York State the next year, 1916,
and other states followed New York's example. American
Indian Day is now celebrated on the fourth Friday in September by most observing states, although some prefer the
second Sunday in May.

By 1915, it was time that the nation should have begun
to think about its Indians. They no longer stood in the way
of the settlers, and the days of their strength were long, long
past. But their names lay across the land: Adirondack and
Connecticut, Monongahela and Allegheny and Ohio, Alabama and Minnesota, Wichita and Tacoma and Yosemite—
some of them modified a bit to fit difficult pronunciations to
a white man's tongue, but still unmistakably Indian. They
have left their words in American speech—mackinaw,
toboggan, hickory, powwow, squaw, moccasin, chipmunk,
raccoon. They had introduced early settlers to new foods and
given them names to call them by—squash, hominy, pem-
mican, succotash—and helped supply pioneer America with
the knowledge of how to survive in a wilderness world.

But unhappily, white man and red were seldom able to
live together in peace. The cause of conflict between them
was too deep and basic: the Indian peoples were in possession of the land and the white men wanted to take it for their
own. With few exceptions, Indian tribes were friendly to the
first white men who came among them to live, until they
learned that the number of settlers would be endless and
their lust for land insatiable. Then, if the Indians tried
to hold what remained to them, there was bloodshed. Even

while they were still on good terms with their new white neighbors, the Indians were not safe, for smallpox, measles, and tuberculosis, caught from the newcomers, decimated and weakened whole tribes, making them incapable of defending themselves.

Tribe after tribe was swept aside by the tide of frontiersmen that began to reach flood proportions after the Revolutionary War, and while some Indians fought back, it was usually an ineffectual resistance. The government again and again made treaties with tribes that stood in the way of the advancing pioneers, getting them to agree to give up their land and move farther west, where they were soon overrun again by the endless waves of land-hungry settlers. Then there was another treaty and another move still farther west.

From time to time, Indian leaders tried to unite independent tribes to defend their lands—men like King Philip (Metacomet), Pontiac, and Tecumseh, who would be celebrated today as great patriots if they had not belonged to a race that was being pushed so remorselessly into the setting sun. But always the Indians' own individuality took away most of the effectiveness of the various confederations: some tribes refused to join; some took the opportunity to pay off old tribal grudges and allied themselves with the whites for the occasion.

The last stand of the Indians was made on the Great Plains, and in the eastern Rockies, where for a score of years the great mounted tribes fought grimly against the United States Cavalry, until at last they went down to weary defeat. These were the leaders on both sides and the battles that have become almost legendary: Chiefs Sitting Bull, Crazy Horse, and Red Cloud; General Nelson A. Miles and Chief Joseph (Hinmaton-Yalaktit); Lieutenant Colonel George Armstrong Custer and the Battle of the Little Big Horn; and General George Crook and Chief Geronimo.

These things, and many more, were what the Indian leader had in mind when, in 1915, he invited all Americans to "celebrate this day and consider our early philosophy, our

102

love of freedom, our social institutions, and our history in the full light of truth . . ."

The diversity of Indian tribes was tremendous. The stereotype Indian is the horseback-riding, buffalo-hunting, tepee-dwelling Sioux or Cheyenne, but no less Indian was the Chippewa in his birchbark canoe, the Iroquois with his fields of corn and squash, the Hopi in his home of rock and adobe, or the Nootka venturing offshore into the Pacific to kill whales.

There were in North America north of Mexico almost 300 tribal languages, with countless dialects, being spoken when the first white men arrived. Scores of tribes have been wiped out by guns or disease in the three centuries since, but today almost 150 of those tribal tongues are still spoken. Some are wistful remnants, known only to a scant dozen or two survivors; others are more than lusty, as the Navaho tongue, known to some 80,000 people, or the Cherokee, spoken by about 50,000.

It is further estimated that there were about 1,100,000 Indians north of Mexico in 1492, about 850,000 of them within the present area of the United States, excluding Alaska. By 1900, there were probably not many more than 250,000 left in the United States and they were so poverty-stricken, so disease-ridden, so without purpose that federal Indian policy was based on the premise that the remaining natives would gradually die off. The phrase, "the Vanishing American," was coined to describe the poignant plight of these people who were fading from the land they had once owned.

But the Vanishing American has refused to vanish. His numbers began increasing again, and, in 1960, the census listed 523,591 in the forty-eight contiguous states. A good many of those were of mixed blood, but remained members of tribes, or for other reasons preferred to call themselves Indian rather than white. In addition, unknown numbers of white Americans carry some degree of Indian blood in their veins.

A considerable part of the tribesmen still live on reservations, and most of them are poor. A few fortunate tribes, however, have become prosperous because oil or minerals have been found on their land, while others have developed special capabilities, like some of the Apaches who have become skilled cattlemen. Indians today—whether they live on or off the reservations—are farmers, ranchers, laborers, mechanics, housewives, and an increasing number are secretaries, nurses, and business and professional men, as more young men and women obtain higher educations. The chief of one large tribe became the urbane, business-suited vice-president of one of the nation's largest petroleum companies.

Many Indian ways and customs are doomed to disappear. The languages spoken by the tinier surviving fragments of tribes are almost gone now; only the old people speak them and the young will listen only to English. The reservations will gradually be abandoned—two or three have been given up in the past few years—but it should be only as the Indians become ready to leave these places of refuge and not because they are forced into a world they are not ready to face.

Some things that go back to the roots of the American heritage will be missed if the day comes when all the Indians' distinctive culture is lost in the great melting-pot process. However, there is still some time before that happens—and it seems unlikely that the time will ever come when the Indians' part in American history will be forgotten.

LEIF ERICSON DAY

(October 9)

MARY F. HOYT

IN THE GREAT HALLS of northern Europe, at the turn of the eleventh century, the *skalds*, or bards, lifted their harps and sang of a wondrous new land. Warm and green, abundantly forested, it was rimmed by wide flat beaches. Plump pink salmon played in its streams, and the deer and quail were plentiful.

The New World lay across the sea—a wind's breath from the straits of Greenland. But it was far different from that rugged, ice-crusted island where the Vikings had settled to farm. It had been discovered, according to the bards, by Leif the Lucky, son of Eric the Red.

The sagas of the Viking explorations to new lands were told to generation after generation. Part myth and part reality, the legends were often embellished to suit the tongue of the storyteller. Yet through the years a strong thread of truth has bound together the story of Leif Ericson. Today, even though debate and speculation over the details of his adventure persist, there is undeniable evidence that indeed he sailed to North America nearly five hundred years before Columbus.

Because Americans traditionally proclaim holidays in remembrance of heroes who have shaped their history, October 9 has been proclaimed Leif Ericson Day. It is a day for all Americans. Just as we try to visualize Columbus, the Italian,

105

touching the shores of the West Indies, or the English Pilgrims landing at Plymouth, we can imagine Leif, the Norseman, first finding the riches of our land.

The ancestors of Leif (it rhymes with safe) sprang from the Nordic tribes of the region that is now called Scandinavia. They were bold, restless men of the sea who went *i viking,* or lurking and raiding, in the fjords, or inlets, of the North. Worshipers of the god Thor, some were barbaric marauders; others were brave warriors.

Leif's grandfather Thorvald, and his father Eric, were hot-tempered, quarrelsome Vikings. Accused of splitting the skull of a neighbor, Thorvald was banished with his family from Norway to Iceland. Years later, the red-bearded Eric fled westward from Iceland for similar reasons. And so young Leif was raised on barren Greenland, deceptively named by his father to attract other Vikings to the narrow band of grazing land on the coast of the glacial island.

As a young Viking, Leif probably learned about his people and his fatherland on *rune stones,* inscriptions carved on stone and wood in the strange, sixteen-character runic alphabet that had not yet been replaced by the Roman alphabet. It is said that he learned the secrets of coastal trading from a foster father—Thryker by name—who taught him the value of silver and gold and how to trade coins for goods. Viking boys also needed to know how to use the sword and spear, to hunt and fish, to carve metal and leather, and to play chess. But most of all, like their elders, their eyes turned to the sea. There they saw the fleets of Viking ships, serpent thin, bristling with oars, their bright square woolen sails billowing behind high-arched prows that were carved into griffin heads. "Studs of the waves" they were called by friends, "dragon ships" by foes.

The sagas which tell of Leif's first journey across the ocean and his subsequent discovery of America were finally written down some three hundred years after the fact, about A.D. 1300; they conflict in some respects. Two records, however, known as the *Hauk's Book* and the *Flatey Book,* agree that about the year 999, when he was twenty years old, Leif set sail for Norway in his own serpent ship. Courageously he set his course directly east to Norway across the wild, open seas. He carried cargo for King Olaf Tryggvesson: sealskins, walrus hides, tusks, and falcons, hooded with leather, for the sport of noblemen.

One of the sagas says that Leif was "big and strong, of striking appearance, shrewd, and in every respect a temperate, fair-dealing man." He was also unafraid of new ideas and, after a winter in Olaf's court under the influence of the King, he was converted to Christianity. When he left for home, a Catholic priest set sail with him, carrying the new religion to the colonists who had migrated to Greenland.

It is at this point—on the eve of Leif's discovery of America—that details in the sagas diverge. No one knows, for example, exactly when or why he became known as "Leif the Lucky." One saga says that the return trip from Norway was harrowing and that Leif's fragile ship, loaded with timber, was thrown off course by a howling gale. Lost, racing perilously fast with the wind, Leif and his crew finally sighted land—after forty days and nights.

The other tale, more acceptable to modern scholars, suggests that another Viking sailor, named Bjarni Herjulfson, had blown off course, and sailed within sight of the shore of America. When Leif returned from Norway, the stories of a new land sparked his curiosity, prompting him to buy Bjarni's boat and set forth on another lucky sea venture.

In reconstructing what took place when Leif discovered the New World in the year A.D. 1000, it seems probable that he first landed in central Labrador, christening it Helluland, or Land of the Flat Stones. Then, continuing south to a warmer, greener spot, he probably landed on southern Labrador or Newfoundland, which he called Markland, or Land of Forests. The exact location of his third landing is still under debate and may have been Cape Cod, Martha's Vineyard, or Long Island. He called this new territory Vinland the Good.

According to legend, Vinland the Good flourished with the bounty of nature; self-sown wheat fields skirted thick groves of the "mausur," evidently a specie of maple. Some say that Vinland was named for the grapes that grew wild near the beaches; some believe that *"vin*land" referred to fertile fields of grass; still others think he was confusing cranberries with grapes.

Leif and his men spent more than a winter in the New World before they sailed home with stories of the warm, good life they had been living. Then other Vikings set sail for America, attempting to colonize—in spite of the hostile *skraelings,* or natives, who had appeared. But Leif never returned to the land he discovered. His devotion to spreading the Christian faith—and the obligations he assumed as leader of Greenland after his father died—precluded further seafaring or exploration.

Modern archaeologists are constantly discovering new bits of evidence to add authenticity and richness to the lore of the Vikings. Recently, in the little fishing village of L'Anse au Meadow, or Bay of Meadow, in Newfoundland, a Viking settlement was uncovered, including the traces of a typical Norse great hall as well as a primitive iron smelter which is dated by radiocarbon to have been in use around A.D. 1000. A Norsewoman's spinning tool, made from a piece of soapstone cooking pot, has been unearthed, the oldest European household artifact yet found in North America.

But sometime later—exactly when we do not know—these first Western settlers in America disappeared. Whether they were killed by the Indians, or whether they returned home to Greenland, or Iceland or Scandinavia, is unknown. And in the following centuries all memory of the first attempt to colonize America faded from the minds of later Scandinavians—save only for the stirring and conflicting sagas about the exploits of Leif the Lucky.

That is why, despite our admiration for the skill and boldness of Leif and his adventurous fellow Vikings, Columbus is remembered as the discoverer of America—because the New

World was not forgotten again after his discovery. It was not Leif's fault that his rich and wonderful Vinland was "lost" by his descendants. And as the search of the archaeologists continues, the past will unfold still further, and someday we shall assuredly know more about Leif Ericson, the European who reached America nearly five hundred years before Columbus.

COLUMBUS DAY

(October 12)

ROBERT G. ALBION

AT TWO O'CLOCK in the morning of October 12, 1492, three
small Spanish ships, the *Niña,* the *Pinta,* and the *Santa
María,* were sailing westward in the Atlantic Ocean, heading
toward one of the great events in history. They had been out
of sight of land since early in September—thirty-three days—
crossing unknown areas of the ocean in search of the East
Indies. Suddenly, the lookout on the little *Pinta* gave the welcome news. "Land! Land!" he cried. His captain, seeing it
too, ordered a gun fired to announce the news to the other
ships.

There was special joy and relief aboard the biggest ship,
the *Santa María,* where the Italian admiral Christopher
Columbus had been growing more and more anxious as day
after day had passed with nothing but water to be seen in
all directions. Two days earlier his crews had become so
restless that he had promised that if land were not sighted
within three days he would turn back. His time had almost
run out. But now his bold dream, his years of search for
money to pay for his voyage, and his skillful navigation had
achieved success. Although he did not know it, he had discovered, not what he was looking for, but a whole new world.

When daylight came, the ships approached the land they
had found, an island in the Bahamas which Columbus
named "San Salvador" (Holy Saviour), probably the present
Watlings Island. He and his men went ashore dressed in

110

their very best. They knelt and thanked God for their safe voyage; then Columbus took possession of the island in the name of Spain.

Columbus, whose Italian name was Cristoforo Colombo, was born in Genoa, Italy, at a time when many people were eager to find an easy way to bring to Europe the spices and silks and other things which were produced in Asia, a long, long distance away. Portuguese explorers discovered that India and China and eastern Asia could be reached by sea, by sailing south around the tip of Africa and heading east from there. But that too was a long journey. It seemed to Columbus that it would be shorter and easier to sail west to the Indies across the Atlantic. Surely it could not be very far around the world in that direction.

Columbus did not invent the idea that the world was round —many educated men already believed that—but he was the first to try to make practical use of the idea. He miscalculated, however, on the size of the earth. Not realizing that the ocean which surrounded Japan was not the same one that was along the shores of Spain, he thought that Japan was only 3,000 miles from Spain, instead of the actual 10,500. After spending many years trying to find someone who would pay for a voyage to the west, he finally won the support of Queen Isabella of Spain. So it was in Spain's name that he took possession of the land he discovered. In subsequent years many others followed the route he had opened up, and the money which Queen Isabella gave to Columbus was returned many times over in the riches which other Spanish captains brought back to Spain.

Columbus went on to explore Cuba and Santo Domingo— Hispaniola, he called it. He made three more voyages; but he found none of the spices and wealth of the Indies for which he was searching, and he never realized that he had not found more islands of groups already known, but had found a new group of islands that lie between two continents, then unknown.

Columbus, who discovered it, deserved to have the new

111

world named for him. However, an Italian explorer, Amerigo Vespucci (Americus Vespucius), who went some time later to explore along the coast of South America, told a thrilling story of his discoveries. A German geographer who was making a map of the new areas heard these stories and he put the name "America" in large letters on the newly found land. So it is that we live in North America rather than North Columbia.

Columbus and his men were not the first men from Europe to reach America. The Vikings from Scandinavia did some exploring along the northern coast some centuries earlier. But no one followed these explorers and even the fact of the exploration was in time forgotten.

October 12 is now celebrated as a holiday throughout North and South America. But such celebration did not begin until many years after the event. It was on the three hundredth anniversary of Columbus' discovery, on October 12, 1792, that the Society of St. Tammany and Columbian Order in New York held a dinner with elaborate ceremonies in honor of the occasion, and dedicated a monument to Christopher Columbus. Shortly thereafter, the government of the newly independent United States named the area where its capital was to be, the District of Columbia. Columbia became a sort of poetic name for the new nation, and its citizens sang of "Columbia, the gem of the ocean," and "Hail, Columbia! happy land!"

The four hundredth anniversary of the discovery, in 1892, was celebrated with more festivities. In New York, at the southwest corner of Central Park, Columbus Circle was built, with a statue of Columbus on a great high pedestal in the middle of it. The following year the great Columbian Exposition was held in Chicago. This was one of the best world's fairs ever held. Replicas of Columbus' three vessels were built in Spain and brought over to be shown there. And a series of postage stamps was issued by the United States government, with pictures of the high points in the Columbus story.

As people began to think more of Columbus, and of his vital importance in the history of the New World, the governor of Colorado proclaimed a statewide observance of Columbus Day in 1905. Gradually other states followed his lead, until it became a legal holiday in more than two thirds of the states. President Franklin D. Roosevelt, in 1937, issued a proclamation designating each October 12 as Columbus Day, saying, "I do invoke the people of the United States to observe the day with appropriate ceremonies in schools, churches, and other suitable places." Likewise in Canada, in Central and South America, in Italy and in Spain, October 12 is now a day to honor the memory of the discoverer of America.

It is entirely fitting that Columbus be so honored, for he had the courage to undertake a voyage which no one else at the time had ever made, confident that he was right in his calculation that by sailing west he would arrive at the land which had always been reached before by traveling east. His discovery of a new world pointed the way for people who would explore it, looking for gold and riches. But much more important than the wealth which they found and took away is the land that was there and that became a home for people of all nations who had the courage to leave their old homes, confident that the new world was a place where they might find freedom.

UNITED NATIONS DAY

(October 24)

RICHARD M. LEIGHTON

THE HEADQUARTERS of the United Nations, on New York's East Side between Forty-second and Forty-eighth Streets, is a majestic spectacle. The great thirty-nine-story Secretariat Building, of gleaming aluminum, blue-green glass, and gray Vermont marble, thrusting a narrow rectangle upward into the New York skyline, is balanced by the low-lying General Assembly, Conference, and Library buildings, which hug an expanse of ground at its feet.

Every year more than 800,000 people come to see these buildings. The great auditorium of the General Assembly, where representatives of more than a hundred nations debate the problems of world peace, is almost half as large as a football field and as high as a seven-story building. It has seats for more than 800 delegates, visiting officials, the press, and the public. Through earphones, a visitor may hear speeches on the floor of the hall translated simultaneously in any of the five official languages of the United Nations: Chinese, English, French, Russian, and Spanish. He may stroll through the handsomely appointed public lounges, purchase United Nations postage stamps and other souvenirs, or admire the round reflecting pool and fountain before the Secretariat Building, with its alternate serpentines of crushed white marble and black pebbles, donated by the children of the United States. He may hear a guide explain how the great

114

gold-plated Foucault Pendulum, a gift of the Netherlands, continuously swings with the earth's rotation.

In the United States and in many other countries, a special day, October 24, is set aside as the official "birthday" of this important world organization. The President of the United States issues a proclamation, urging all United States citizens, communities, government officials, and organizations to commemorate the occasion with special programs. In Canada, the Prime Minister issues a similar statement. Several countries observe a United Nations Week.

Like many other dates commemorated as holidays, October 24, 1945, did not seem especially memorable at the time. In Washington, D.C., on that day the weather was moderately cool, rather cloudy, with occasional sun. Almost eight weeks had passed since the news of Japan's surrender had brought jubilant throngs into the streets and parks around the White House. Time had begun to blur both the mood and the memory. Now our soldiers were coming home from Europe and the Pacific by the hundreds of thousands—unfortunately leaving unfinished business behind. In every American community there were reunions with fathers, husbands, brothers, and sons. Factories were reconverting, scrambling for scarce materials and machinery; men just out of uniform, or still in them, were looking for jobs; strikes were erupting; prices were pushing through the loopholes of wartime controls still in force.

Newspaper headlines were grim. In eastern Europe, Greece, Iran, and Korea, the Communists were either in full control or threatening to take over. The first of a series of foreign ministers' conferences in London had failed to work out postwar differences with the Russians. Congress was debating ways to keep the "secrets" of manufacturing the atomic bomb. And President Truman had asked for one year of compulsory military training for all eighteen-year-old youths.

In this atmosphere in Washington, on that afternoon of October 24, 1945, one event passed almost unnoticed.

115

Shortly after three o'clock, a subordinate official of the Soviet Embassy delivered to the State Department the ratification, or approval, of the Charter of the United Nations from his government and from the Russian republics of Byelorussia and Ukrainia. These formalities were in accordance with the provisions of the Charter itself, which had been drawn up the preceding spring at a great international conference held in San Francisco and attended by fifty nations representing most of the civilized world warring with Germany and Japan. They had decided that the United Nations would come into force only after its Charter had been ratified by all the governments of the wartime "Big Five" (United States, Soviet Union, United Kingdom, France, and China) as well as by a majority of the remaining small ones. To these, the "Little Forty-five," was later added a forty-sixth, Poland, which had not been represented at San Francisco. During the summer, the ratifications had trickled into Washington. The United States Senate, which had rejected the League of Nations Covenant after World War I, had approved the Charter after a short debate and with only two dissenting votes. And so by October 24, twenty-six nations, including four of the "Big Five," had ratified. Thus, when the Soviet Union and Byelorussia and Ukrainia embraced the ideals of the Charter, a majority was reached and the United Nations was born. Two years later, the General Assembly declared that October 24 would be its official "birthday."

The United Nations Charter is, in a sense, a kind of "declaration of independence"—an effort to end the tyranny and oppression resulting from a world ruled only by force, and to create a new and freer world where all nations assume responsibility for one another. The Charter's preamble opens with a resounding declaration which, to Americans, has a familiar ring:

> *We, the peoples of the United Nations, determined to save succeeding generations from the scourge of war . . . have resolved to combine our efforts to accomplish these aims. . . .*

Accordingly, our respective Governments, through representatives assembled in the city of San Francisco . . . have agreed to the present Charter of the United Nations and do hereby establish an international organization to be known as the United Nations.

Actually the Charter may be likened even more to a constitution. Americans can immediately recognize the similarity, in words and spirit, to their own Constitution: "We, the people of the United States, in order to form a more perfect union . . . do ordain and establish . . ." The Charter is indeed the "constitution" of the United Nations, and its signing by the delegates at San Francisco on June 26, 1945, had much the same significance as had the signing of the draft of the United States Constitution by the delegates to the Constitutional Convention at Philadelphia on September 17, 1787. The delegates on both occasions were architects, not builders, of a new order. Only the governments they represented could translate their blueprints into reality. Only the future would show whether their dreams could be fulfilled.

Today, many of the bright hopes the United Nations once inspired seem to have faded. It has not become a world government with supreme powers and armed forces ample to keep the peace; it has not saved this generation from the scourge of war, nor even deterred powerful nations from dominating and threatening their weaker neighbors. Wars and revolutions have erupted often since 1945: China, Korea, and Indochina; Greece, Algeria, Cyprus, Laos, Egypt, Cuba, Tibet, Vietnam, and many other places. America spends 50 billions of dollars each year to keep its defenses strong, and still nuclear war perils the world.

But if the United Nations has not eliminated war, it has at least curbed it. In 1948 and 1949, the United Nations successfully intervened to stop hostilities between the Dutch and their former colony of Indonesia. The year following, forty-one countries rallied under the blue flag of the United Nations to hurl back the Communist invaders of South

Korea, and UN forces are policing that country's border with North Korea today.

In the Suez crisis of 1956, when Israeli, French, and British forces attacked Egypt following the latter's seizure of the Suez Canal, it was the UN General Assembly that brought about a cease-fire and establishment of a United Nations Emergency Force to supervise withdrawal of foreign troops and preserve peace. And for four years, special multinational forces under United Nations command maintained a precarious peace in the primitive backcountry of the Congo after the termination of Belgian rule in 1960.

The International Atomic Energy Agency, a UN body, was established in 1957 to implement President Eisenhower's atoms-for-peace program. Through its various agencies, the United Nations carries out programs of technical and financial assistance and development for underdeveloped countries, helps refugees, provides food and medical care for children, conducts research in manifold areas of human need, sponsors international disarmament negotiations, operates international mediation and conciliation services, administers former colonial territories in trust, and maintains the International Court of Justice. The Secretary General of the United Nations, in his role of international mediator and "troubleshooter" in many crises, has become a potent instrument of peace in a troubled world.

ELECTION DAY

(*First Tuesday after the First Monday in November*)

MARTIN BLUMENSON

UNLIKE PEOPLE in many other countries, American citizens
have the right to elect their political leaders. In our representative democracy, all citizens fulfilling certain require-
ments are free to choose the men and women who will represent them in the government. They make their choices by
voting.

The rules on who may vote vary from one state to another,
for each state has the authority under the Constitution to
prescribe the voters' qualifications. In general, a citizen may
vote if he is an adult, if he has lived in the community for a
specified length of time, if he has committed no serious
crime, if he is mentally sound, and if he has proved his
eligibility to vote by *registering* in his locality in advance of
the election. However, some states now allow new residents
to vote in *Presidential elections* if they are registered else-
where.

Elections take place on several levels in the United States,
officials being elected for national, state, county, and munic-
ipal governments. The officials are usually elected from
among the candidates presented by each *political party* on a
list called a *slate* or a *ticket*. Each party presents its philosophy, program, and promises to the voters by means of a
platform, and each provision in the platform is called a
plank. Although most candidates run on the Republican or

119

Democratic Party ticket, some belong to other parties, while others with no party affiliation run as Independents.

When voters register, they may express their preference for a political party. In some states this gives them the right to vote in the *primary* election in order to help select the candidates of their party. In other states the political parties choose their candidates by meeting in convention. In the *general* election, all the voters regardless of party and comprising the *electorate* make their choices by voting for the candidates they prefer.

Before an election the candidates conduct *campaigns* to seek the support of the voters. The campaign is very important, not only to the voters but also to the candidates who are working to get elected. The candidates debate the important issues of the day, each trying to convince the electorate that his proposed solutions to current problems are preferable to those of his opponents. They may appear on television, speak on street corners and over the radio, and purchase advertisements in the newspapers. In various other ways each tries to persuade the voters that he is honest, knowledgeable, responsive to their wishes, and deserving of their votes.

Political campaigns sometimes have a carnival air about them. Sound trucks cruise through the streets playing music and blaring forth the voices of the candidates. Garish election posters are plastered on walls. Candidates try to look handsome and sincere; there is much handshaking, backslapping, and baby-kissing. Supporters stage parades, sing songs, and carry banners. All this generates a mounting excitement and suspense as Election Day approaches.

But these aspects of the campaign do not obscure the fact that an election is a serious business. It is one of the most important processes in a democracy. And the voter should listen carefully to the campaign promises and think hard on the *issues* he will help decide by his vote. After making thoughtful comparisons of party platforms and candidates, he should exercise his independent judgment in deciding for whom he should vote on Election Day.

Election Day

A citizen votes in the *precinct* where he lives. The precinct is a voting district, an area small enough for the convenience of both the voters and the election officials. The voting place, or the *polls*, is some centrally located building: a firehouse, a police station, a school, or a store—and the American flag is always displayed there on Election Day. The place, as well as the hours that the polls will remain open to the voters, is announced in advance in the local newspapers. Usually the polls are open from 7:00 A.M. until 7:00 P.M. Many employers give their employees time off from work to enable them to vote, and in some states the law requires them to do so.

At the polls the voter identifies himself to the election officials. If he is officially registered, he receives an official *ballot,* printed at government expense, which carries the names of the candidates who are running for office. It also has blank spaces so that if the voter does not approve of the candidates listed, he may write in the name of anyone he wishes.

The voter casts a *secret ballot,* sometimes called the Australian ballot because the practice originated in that country in 1854. In a booth or screened compartment, alone and undisturbed, he marks his ballot with a pen or pencil, indicating his choice of the competing candidates. When finished, the voter folds his ballot so that no one can see how he has voted, returns to the main room at the polls, and places his ballot in the *ballot box,* which is locked so that no one can tamper with the votes that have been deposited.

Election officials are responsible for preventing unauthorized persons from putting ballots in the box—or "stuffing the ballot box." Helping them are people appointed by the political parties as *watchers.* Many precincts use *voting machines,* on which the voter turns appropriate handles to mark his ballot. These machines are kept locked and are treated exactly like the ballot boxes.

After the polls are closed, the election officials, in the presence of the party watchers, open the ballot box, count the votes, and report the totals cast for each candidate. They also count the *absentee ballots,* those votes cast by citizens

121

who are ill, out of the country, in the armed forces, or otherwise unable to visit the polls. When the results are tallied, those candidates receiving the most votes are certified as having been elected to the offices for which they ran.

There are sometimes unscrupulous persons who try to win elections by immoral means in order to gain power for their own selfish ends. To combat them, the states have passed laws to prevent election abuses and frauds. These laws prescribe penalties for those who try to purchase votes, bribe, intimidate, or threaten voters.

In a *direct* election the people vote for their own representatives, while in an *indirect* election the people elect delegates who are empowered to choose the officials. Members of Congress are elected directly, although before the Seventeenth Amendment was added to the Constitution in 1913, members of the United States Senate were chosen indirectly by elected state officials who were authorized to elect the senators.

The election of the President and Vice-President of the United States is indirect in form, although direct in practice. The framers of the Constitution, who wished to remove the election of the two highest offices in the land from partisan politics, arranged to have the voters elect members of an *Electoral College,* expecting that these *Electors* would be senior statesmen who would choose the two best men for President and Vice-President regardless of political party. Today Americans make these choices themselves, voting for Electors who have pledged to vote in the Electoral College for the candidates of a specific party.

The President and Vice-President are elected for a *term* of four years. Senators are elected for terms of six years, one-third of them being elected every two years. Representatives are elected for two-year terms.

There was no single Election Day in the United States until 1845, when Congress designated the first Tuesday after the first Monday in November, every fourth year, as the date for choosing the Electoral College. In 1872, the Congress

122

fixed the same date in every even year for electing the members of the House of Representatives—except in Maine, because the constitution of that state specified the second Monday in September as Election Day and the Congress did not want to interfere. The Seventeenth Amendment also designated the November date for the direct election of senators, again except for Maine.

Thus, Americans vote on Election Day in November every four years for the Electors who will meet during the following month in their state capitals to select the President and Vice-President of the United States. They vote every two years on the same date in November (except in Maine) to choose their representatives and one-third of their senators. And in many states Americans also vote on Election Day for their state and local officials.

Voting in America is not compulsory. It is a privilege of citizenship. To deny this right to any citizen is to deny complete freedom for all citizens. The right to vote is a basic aim of the Civil Rights demonstrations which began and grew throughout the United States in the 1960's.

On Election Day, the millions of Americans who exercise their right to vote are participating in their own self-government and are thereby ensuring the responsiveness of the government to the will of the people.

123

VETERANS' DAY

(Formerly Armistice Day, November 11)

GUNTHER E. ROTHENBERG

ACROSS THE POTOMAC, facing the nation's capital and the Lincoln Memorial, lies Arlington National Cemetery. Here amid the rolling Virginia hills are the graves of some 120,000 veterans, the famous and the obscure alike. In the approximate center of the cemetery, on a terrace commanding a fine view of Washington across the river, stands an austerely simple monument, the Tomb of the Unknowns, guarded day and night by an armed sentry. In a crypt below the single fifty-ton block of white marble rest the bodies of three American soldiers, all unknown, representing the dead of three wars—World Wars I and II and the Korean conflict. Every November 11, Veterans' Day, a Presidential wreath is laid here in a solemn ceremony.

November 11 was chosen because the date marks the end of World War I. On that day, one hour before noon, firing ceased along the battle line in France. Slowly soldiers climbed out of their trenches and rifle pits, first with some apprehension, then with mounting excitement and relief. The war was over! After nearly four and a half years of bloody fighting, the armies of the Western Allies—above all those of France, Great Britain, and the United States—finally had beaten the mighty military machinery of imperial Germany and her allies. Emperor William II, to many the symbol of hated autocracy, had fled the country, and on November 10 the new German government unconditionally accepted the Allied armistice terms.

The United States under President Woodrow Wilson had entered World War I on April 6, 1917, in order to defend certain basic American positions then threatened by Germany and her allies. American war aims, spelled out in Wilson's famous Fourteen Points, included the principles of freedom of the seas, the right for people everywhere to determine their own government and, above all, the establishment of a League of Nations to secure a lasting peace for all mankind. It was for such high ideals that over 50,000 Americans laid down their lives and more than 200,000 were wounded.

To be sure, America's allies suffered far more grievous losses, but the American contribution was decisive. After knocking Russia out of the war late in 1917, Germany hoped to strike a final blow against the weary French and English forces in the west. American troops, so the German High Command asserted, would never get to France in sufficient numbers to change the outcome. But, escorted by the United States Navy, powerful contingents arrived in France early in 1918. In the first days of June, American troops turned back the spearhead of the last German drive on Paris, and in late September over 1,200,000 "doughboys" took part in the Meuse-Argonne offensive which broke the German lines. By the time of the armistice, over two million Americans were serving under General John J. Pershing in the American Expeditionary Force.

The end of the war was celebrated in Paris and London with a great outburst of joy. In the United States, with a time differential of six hours on the east coast, news that the war was over was released at 2:45 A.M. By breakfast time the news had flashed throughout the country and thousands poured into churches and synagogues to offer thanks. All across the land people celebrated. Ticker tape covered the avenues of the big cities and after the passing of the first, spontaneous celebrations, Americans began to think about creating a permanent memorial. President Wilson expressed these feelings in his Armistice Day proclamation of 1919: "To us in America," he said, "the reflections of Armistice Day will be filled with solemn pride in the heroism of those who died in the country's service and with gratitude for the victory . . ."

To show this gratitude, and as a symbolic honor for all of the nation's dead in the conflict, it was decided to bring the body of an unidentified American soldier home from the battlefields and to rebury him in Arlington National Cemetery. From American war cemeteries in France, four unidentified bodies were brought to the City Hall of Châlons-sur-Marne where Sergeant Edward S. Younger, the most decorated enlisted man of World War I, made the final choice. After praying for divine guidance, he placed a spray of white roses on one of the unmarked caskets.

The United States cruiser *Olympia* returned the body to its native land, and on November 11, 1921, President Warren G. Harding, his Cabinet, representatives of the armed services, diplomats from many nations, and thousands of somber citizens watched the flag-draped caisson bear the body to the cemetery. At precisely 11:00 A.M., the Unknown Soldier was laid to his final rest in the crypt below the marble marker which bears the inscription:

> HERE RESTS IN HONORED GLORY
> AN AMERICAN SOLDIER
> KNOWN BUT TO GOD.

Thereafter, Armistice Day was commemorated each year in ceremonies at the tomb, while in all other parts of the country the American Legion (founded by World War I veterans), as well as other patriotic groups, sponsored parades and memorial services. At exactly two minutes before the hour of eleven all traffic came to a halt, business was suspended, and classes were interrupted while Americans paid silent tribute to the dead of the Great War. In 1927, President Calvin Coolidge, at the request of Congress, issued a proclamation urging government officials and citizens to observe the occasion with special programs in their communities. A decade later, on May 15, 1938, President Franklin D. Roosevelt signed a bill declaring Armistice Day a legal holiday. In France, England, and the British Empire, too, Armistice Day was commemorated with solemn ceremonies.

By 1938, however, the promise of a world "safe for democracy," for which America had fought in World War I, was rapidly disappearing. In the Far East and in Europe, aggressors were again on the move. World War II started in Europe in September, 1939, and after the Japanese attack on Pearl Harbor on December 7, 1941, the United States was once more at war.

During the next four years an ever increasing number of American soldiers, sailors, airmen, and marines fought on the far-flung fronts of a global war. Nearly 15 million men and women served in uniform and American war dead were buried, not only in Europe but also in North Africa, in Asia, and on the islands of the Pacific. The cause of the United States and her allies prevailed. Italy gave up in 1943; Germany surrendered on May 7, 1945; and after atomic bombs were dropped on Hiroshima and Nagasaki, the Japanese government asked for peace on August 10, 1945.

Again Americans celebrated victory and believed that a prosperous and peaceful world was secured. But again such hopes proved in vain. Within a few months after the end of the war, the Western democracies (led by the United States) and the Communist world (led by the Soviet Union) found themselves bitterly divided. The Cold War began and America realized reluctantly that she would have to maintain considerable armed strength in a dangerous world. Just how dangerous was revealed on June 25, 1950, when soldiers from Communist North Korea invaded South Korea, opening a drawnout conflict which lasted until 1953 and took the lives of over 33,000 Americans.

To many millions of World War II and Korean veterans,

127

Armistice Day, which was specifically dedicated to the remembrance of World War I, had little personal meaning.
Therefore leaders of various veterans' organizations combined to transform the day into an occasion honoring *all*
the 31 million Americans who had fought in the nation's
wars. On November 11, 1953, a Veterans' Day observance
was held in Emporia, Kansas, and in February of the following year Congressman Edward J. Rees offered a bill in Congress to change the name of Armistice Day to Veterans' Day.
The bill promptly passed the House and the Senate and on
June 1, 1954, President Dwight D. Eisenhower, former Supreme Commander of Allied Forces in Europe, signed into
law an act "to honor veterans on the eleventh day of November each year."

Four years later, the bodies of two more Unknown American Soldiers were placed in the crypt in Arlington. Aboard
the cruiser *Canberra,* Hospitalman First Class William R.
Charette, holder of the Medal of Honor, chose the body representing the dead of World War II from two coffins, one from
the European and the other from the Pacific Theater of
Operations. At the same time Master Sergeant Ned Lyle,
United States Army, chose the Unknown of the Korean conflict from four caskets at the National Cemetery in Hawaii.
On May 30, 1958, the bodies were buried in Arlington. President Eisenhower placed a Medal of Honor on each casket
and cannon boomed a twenty-one-gun salute.

And so they lie in Arlington, the three Unknowns, symbolizing the honored dead of a nation which believes in
peace, but which is prepared to fight in defense of freedom
and liberty. This is the dual significance of Veterans' Day,
celebrated in all the states of the Union and in all territories
under the Stars and Stripes. November 11 is an occasion not
only to honor the veterans of past wars and to pay tribute to
the dead, but it is also a day dedicated to the hope that their
sacrifices will not have been in vain.

DISCOVERY DAY

(November 19)

EARL   PARKER   HANSON

ON NOVEMBER 19, 1493, Christopher Columbus touched the shores of a lush, green island in the Lesser Antilles to replenish his water supply. He was on his second voyage to the New World, claiming islands in the name of Ferdinand and Isabella of Spain. Columbus and his men, among whom was Juan Ponce de León, were greeted by friendly Indians in a village built around a "plaza," who told him that the island was called Borinquén. Before he sailed away, Columbus claimed the island for the Castile, renaming it San Juan Bautista—for St. John the Baptist, although perhaps also in honor of Prince Juan, heir to the Spanish throne.

In 1508, Ponce de León returned to the island and established a permanent colony near a fine sailing port which he called Porto Rico, or Rich Port. Through the years, by some trick of fate, or a cartographer's error, these names were inverted: the city became known as San Juan and the island took the name Puerto Rico.

Each year on November 19, the people of Puerto Rico observe the day that they became an "official" part of the New World. This is their "Discovery Day," and special ceremonies are held in the Plaza de Colón in San Juan. On this day the people on the "mainland" of the United States may well remember the unique history of the vigorous little commonwealth.

129

From 1508 until 1898, Puerto Rico remained a Spanish colony. Then on July 25, 1898, in the course of the Spanish-American War, Army General Nelson A. Miles landed with his troops and inaugurated United States rule over the island.

The United States installed a civil government in 1900, with a legislature to which the Puerto Ricans elected their own representatives. But this body had almost no power, for the United States governor of Puerto Rico and the members of his cabinet, who were appointed by the President of the United States with the consent of the United States Senate, could set aside laws that the Puerto Rican legislature passed. The governing of the island was in fact done by a small office in Washington, acting through the governor.

Although the Puerto Rican people were offered—and accepted—United States citizenship in 1917, the island in effect remained a colony without control of its own destiny. The sugar industry flourished, but the rest of the economy stagnated. The worldwide depression and a rapidly increasing population resulted in unemployment, starvation, and despair. Soon a drive for independence stirred among the islanders.

Out of the restless population arose a new leader, Luis Muñoz Marín, organizer of the Popular Democratic Party, the PPD, which won the election of 1940 and has been in power ever since. He reasoned that the improvement of Puerto Rico's political status could wait, that the big job was to lift his people from poverty. With the help of Governor Rexford Tugwell, appointed by President Franklin D. Roosevelt for the purpose, Muñoz Marín and his colleagues began to work for economic, social, and cultural progress—and with these, step by step, came emancipation from colonialism. On July 25, 1952, exactly fifty-four years after the landing of the Marines, Puerto Rico, by decision of its own people and consent of the United States, received its present status as a commonwealth or "free associated state."

As citizens of the United States, Puerto Ricans enjoy all the civil rights enjoyed by other American citizens and are fully protected, everywhere, under the American flag and laws. Although subject to the military draft, they pay no federal taxes and they cannot vote for the President of the United States.

In the last twenty years Puerto Rico's economic and social improvement has accelerated dramatically. "Operation Bootstrap" has been developed to multiply jobs and wages and improve living standards through better education, public health facilities, and other services. "Operation Commonwealth" has resulted in improvements in political status. And "Operation Serenity"—a government program unique in all the world—seeks through encouragement of art, learning, and all human creativity to make economic growth a means to greater freedom and knowledge, not as an end in itself. Particular emphasis is placed on the Spanish origin of the island's culture.

Each year more than a thousand visitors come to Puerto Rico from all over the world to study the island's progress. Annual individual income has risen from an average of $121 in 1940 to $830 today. Illiteracy has been reduced from a figure of nearly 50 per cent of the population in 1940 to 11 per cent; and the death rate, which was eighteen per thousand now stands at six per thousand per year, below that in the United States.

Side by side with the economic and social improvements, an impressive cultural renaissance has taken place. Puerto Rican painters, composers, poets, and novelists are making impressive contributions to the world of art and the island's cultural life. Native folk songs have become increasingly popular and, for the sophisticated, the world-famous Spanish cellist Pablo Casals and the annual music festival that bears his name draw audiences from many countries.

As a commonwealth, Puerto Rico's relationship with the United States is unlike that of the fifty federated states. Only the United States Supreme Court—and that only on constitutional grounds—may set aside laws passed by the Puerto Rican legislature; the American Congress has voluntarily relinquished that power. The United States handles foreign affairs affecting the island, manages the armed forces, runs the Post Office, and carries out federal programs—in housing and agriculture, for instance—precisely as it does in the fifty states. Similarly, Puerto Rico receives grants-in-aid from the federal government for building roads, old-age assistance, free lunches for schoolchildren, and the like.

If Puerto Rico ever chooses independence in place of its present commonwealth status, it will lose the free trade which it now enjoys with the United States, free entry for sugar and other products shipped to the mainland. And if it becomes a federated state, it will have to pay United States federal taxes as the other states do. In view of the island's lack of natural resources, most Puerto Ricans fear that either course would spell ruin. And so their choice is to remain a commonwealth, which for them offers promise for a richer future.

It is important to remember that Puerto Rico's commonwealth status was not "won" by the Puerto Ricans nor "granted" by the United States Congress. It resulted from cooperation between the two, and it is an outstanding example of what can happen when a great power collaborates with its former colonial peoples, in a spirit of friendship and for the mutual benefit of both.

It is also important to remember that when Columbus landed on Puerto Rico he touched for the first and the last time what is now United States territory. This event, celebrated on Discovery Day, also strengthens the bond between our peoples.

THANKSGIVING DAY

(Fourth Thursday in November)

MAX SAVELLE

THANKSGIVING is America's most typical, most distinctively American holiday. Other nations have holidays that are like our Fourth of July; many nations celebrate Christmas and New Year's Day; and many celebrate the birthdays of their national heroes. But only a very few have days of national thanksgiving.

The idea of giving thanks is neither new nor peculiarly American. The ancient Hebrew Feast of Tabernacles (Succoth) is a thanksgiving and harvest festival. The Greeks, too, had a harvest festival, their Feast of Demeter, goddess of agriculture; and the Romans celebrated Cerealia, honoring their goddess Ceres. But the immediate forerunner of the American Thanksgiving was the old English "harvest home," with its church service of thanksgiving for the harvest, followed by a public feast and sports. This was a very common holiday in the England of the first colonizers of Anglo-America.

It was quite customary for colonists arriving in America to render thanks to God for their safe arrival. The trip from Europe in the small sailing ships of the time was long and difficult; and it must have been a welcome feeling indeed to set foot on land once more. In "Berkeley Hundred," a private subcolony in Virginia, colonists landed early in December, 1619. At once they celebrated a day of thanksgiving for their

133

safe arrival and, under the terms of their charter, proclaimed that day, December 4, as a day of thanksgiving to be observed every year.

Traditionally, however, the Thanksgiving which we celebrate today has usually been considered to have its origin in the famous Thanksgiving celebration at Plymouth in the summer of 1621. The Pilgrims had come to Plymouth from England, in search of a place where they might practice their own religion, a right that was denied to them in England. They had landed on the cold shore of Massachusetts in November of 1620, tired and many of them sick after their long voyage. It was a long, cold winter such as they had never known, and many of them perished. But those who survived managed to cut down trees and drag them by hand, since they had no horses, and to build for themselves neat, warm houses to live in and a blockhouse, or wooden fort, for their protection.

There had been no threat to the Pilgrims that winter from the Indians, for they had made a treaty with the great chief Massasoit, which gave them peace, a peace that lasted for fifty years. But they had had to combat a very real threat of starvation, for they had brought barely enough food to last them through the first spring and summer. They had all too good a reason to plant their corn carefully that spring as the Indians taught them, and then to sit up nights, watching, to keep the wolves from digging up the fish they used for fertilizer!

The first year was thus for them a life-and-death struggle. It is no wonder that when a bountiful harvest of corn had been reaped and stored away they should have felt an outburst of joy, and a desire to give thanks and celebrate their safe deliverance from the critical dangers through which they had passed. They invited the Indians to come and help them celebrate, which the savages were happy to do, bringing with them five deer to add to the feast.

Edward Winslow, one of the leaders of the colony, described the Pilgrim Thanksgiving thus:

Thanksgiving Day

Our harvest being gotten in, our governor [William Bradford] sent four men on fowling, that so we might after a special manner rejoice together, after we had gathered the fruit of our labors. They four in one day killed as much fowl as, with a little help beside, served the Company almost a week. At which time, amongst other recreations, we exercised our arms, many of the Indians coming amongst us, and amongst the rest their greatest king, Massasoit with some ninety men, whom for three days we entertained and feasted. And they went out and killed five deer which they brought to the plantation and bestowed on our governor and upon the captain and others.*

But the little colony was not yet free of the danger of starvation; and two years later this danger came perilously near to reality in the long drought of the summer of 1623. Week after week, that summer, they watched their corn withering away for lack of water, and, at last, their governor set aside a day of prayer for a rain that might save their lives. One entire day they prayed; early the next morning it began to rain, and it rained for nearly two weeks. Their crop was saved; never again, thereafter, were they in any real danger of starvation. The governor proclaimed a day of thanksgiving for the lifesaving rain.

After 1623, thanksgiving days were celebrated irregularly, although the General Court of Massachusetts, the state legislature, on November 15, 1636, enacted a law empowering the governor and council to proclaim days of fasting or of thanksgiving whenever "an occasion shall be offered." Similarly, the General Assembly of Virginia in 1624 had proclaimed the day of March 22 an annual thanksgiving day in recognition of their delivery from the Indian massacre of 1622 and the war that followed it. By the middle of the

* Quoted in William Bradford. *Of Plymouth Plantation, 1620–1647,* edited by Samuel E. Morison (New York: Alfred A. Knopf, Inc., 1959), p. 90, fn. 8.

eighteenth century, Thanksgiving had become an annual holiday in Massachusetts, and a generally accepted day for family reunions and celebrations.

The first national Thanksgiving Day came after another great crisis in American history. It was proclaimed by George Washington in 1789. The United States had just passed through the double crisis of War for Independence from England and the struggle for union among thirteen independent and semihostile states. Times were hard after the war; the central government was demoralized and powerless; and the young states were quarreling with one another. But the thirteen erstwhile Colonies rewrote their Constitution and built a stable central government. By the spring of 1789, despite the pessimism of a few years before, there was a condition of order, prosperity, and hope.

It was with a profound sense of divine guidance and deep feeling of gratitude for deliverance from great national danger that Washington proclaimed a day of thanksgiving. He recommended that the citizens thank God for the divine care during the formative Colonial period, for aid during their struggle to be free, for peace and prosperity that had come to the nation since the war, and, most especially, for the new Constitution for the whole nation, which guaranteed to all, the blessings of peace, order, and civil and religious liberty.

In 1846, Mrs. Sarah Josepha Hale, editor of the most important women's magazine of the time, *Godey's Lady's Book*, started a campaign for the regular observance of Thanksgiving Day. As a result, state after state officially adopted the last Thursday of November as an annual day of Thanksgiving, until in 1858 there were only six states that did not observe the custom.

Then came the Civil War, testing whether the nation established in 1789 was to survive or to be divided again into states. Early in 1862, President Lincoln called for a national thanksgiving, to be celebrated in the churches, for the victories of the Northern armies in the Mississippi Valley, and for the avoidance of foreign intervention. The next year, on July 15, 1863, just after the tide of Confederate invasion had been turned back at Gettysburg, he proclaimed August 6 a special day of thanksgiving for the salvation of the Union, and for the newborn hope that the cause of unity must eventually win against the forces of disunion.

Just a few weeks later, Lincoln again called upon the people to render thanks to God, this time for all the blessings of that year, 1863. Peace had been maintained with other nations, crops were good, and the tide of war had definitely turned in favor of the Northern armies. For all these things, but most of all for the preservation of the Union, he called upon the people to be thankful.

This proclamation set aside the last Thursday in November as the national Thanksgiving Day in 1863. The next year, 1864, as the war was drawing to a close, the last Thursday in November was designated again. In 1865, President Andrew Johnson continued the precedent. From that time, the last Thursday in November was set aside as the national Thanksgiving Day every year, first by the President and then by the governors of the states. In 1939, President Franklin D. Roosevelt, because of the short period between the last Thursday of November and Christmas, set the third Thursday of November as the national Thanksgiving. But the outcry from traditionalists over this precedent-shattering move was such that in December, 1941, Congress, by a joint resolution approved by President Roosevelt, provided that the official national Thanksgiving Day should always be the fourth Thursday in November.

BILL OF RIGHTS DAY

(*December 15*)

MARTIN BLUMENSON

THROUGHOUT HISTORY man has endeavored to secure and protect individual rights against tyrannical kings and dictatorial governments. When King John of England signed the Magna Carta in 1215, he agreed to honor certain rights and privileges belonging to the feudal lords, and the nobles in turn conceded certain rights to the people—among them, the rights to justice, to a fair trial if accused of a crime, and to equitable taxation. The Magna Carta deprived the king of absolute power over his subjects and guaranteed certain rights to the people.

In 1689, the English Parliament adopted a Bill of Rights to limit once again the power of the king. This law prohibited the king from suspending laws passed by Parliament, levying taxes without the consent of Parliament, keeping a standing army large enough to subjugate and terrorize the population, abolishing the right of the people to have weapons for their self-defense, preventing the people from petitioning the king to correct governmental abuses, and doing away with free elections and open trials.

An English philosopher, John Locke, explained the relationship between those who govern and those who are governed in a book published in 1690. The people, Locke said, have certain rights they can give to the government—for example, the right to levy taxes and declare war; but there are other rights they cannot give away or have taken away, and these he called "inalienable" rights. Almost one hundred years later, when Thomas Jefferson was writing the American Declaration of Independence, he echoed Locke's words —"all men," Jefferson wrote, "are endowed by their Creator with certain unalienable rights," inalienable rights that cannot be disregarded, violated, or abolished by the government.

In France, too, where men were seeking to establish the rights of citizens, Jean Jacques Rousseau maintained that a compact exists between the people and their government, a contractual agreement that forbids the government from ignoring the rights of individuals. The French Revolution of 1789 produced a document called the Declaration of the Rights of Man, which proclaimed the right of the people to freedom and liberty.

When the English colonies in America announced their independence from England in 1776, they drew up state constitutions. Most of these included separate bills of rights sections, which guaranteed citizens' rights against state action. Other state constitutions, without separate bills of rights, contained similar guarantees of civil liberties in the body of the document.

In their struggle for independence, when the states banded together to form the United States, they created first a constitution called the Articles of Confederation. Fearful of a strong central government, the framers of the Articles of Confederation so limited the powers of the national government that it was too weak to operate effectively. To rectify the deficiencies, the Constitution of the United States was drafted to establish a strong central government. The Constitution guaranteed many individual rights—for example, it prohibited unjust imprisonment, titles of nobility, and religious tests for public officials. But many Americans, having revolted against what they considered to be the tyranny of the English government, and having as a result formed a weak government under the Articles of Confederation, feared that the Constitution gave the central government too much power. They were concerned because the Constitution did not seem adequately to protect the rights of the individual citizen.

In order to gain acceptance for the Constitution and to have the states ratify the document, the framers promised to add a Bill of Rights. When the first Congress met, therefore, James Madison introduced twelve amendments designed to insure the protection of all citizens against the power of the central government. The states ratified ten of these provisions, and these first ten amendments to the Constitution became part of the supreme law of the land on December 15, 1791. They are known as the American Bill of Rights.

The amendments are quite clear:

(1) Congress shall pass no law to establish a state religion or to prohibit any religious worship; no law shall deny freedom of speech and of the press, or the right to assemble peaceably, or the right to petition the government.

(2) All citizens shall have the right to own and bear weapons for their self-protection.

(3) No soldier shall be quartered in anyone's house —in peace, without the consent of the owner or, in war, without due process of law.

(4) There shall be no unreasonable searches and seizures of persons, effects, and houses.

(5) No person shall be tried for a crime unless he has first been indicted by a grand jury, and he shall not be tried for the same crime more than once (double jeopardy), or compelled to testify against himself (self-incrimination), or have his property taken for public use without just compensation, or be deprived of life, liberty, or property without due process of law.

(6) A person accused of a crime shall have the right to a public and speedy trial by jury in the place where the crime was committed; he shall have the right to be confronted by the witnesses against him, to obtain witnesses in his defense, and to have a lawyer help defend him.

(7) In common-law suits, where the matter in controversy has a value of more than twenty dollars, the parties shall have the right to demand a trial by jury.

(8) There shall be no excessive bail or fines, no cruel or unusual punishments.

(9) The enumeration of certain rights in the Constitution and its amendments shall not deny or disparage other rights held by the people.

(10) The powers not delegated to the federal government by the Constitution, nor prohibited to the states, shall be reserved to the states or to the people.

Most of the framers of the Constitution had believed these safeguards were implicit in the Constitution of the United States; the Bill of Rights made them clear and explicit. The Bill of Rights guaranteed certain rights and forbade the Congress to pass laws violating these civil liberties.

Four other amendments to the Constitution, although not part of the Bill of Rights, protect and guarantee other rights: the Thirteenth, prohibiting slavery, gives every person the right to personal freedom; the Fourteenth forbids the states to deprive anyone of life, liberty, or property without due process of law, and prohibits the states from denying anyone the equal protection of the laws; the Fifteenth prevents the states from denying citizens the right to vote because of race or color; and the Nineteenth states that women cannot be denied the right to vote because of their sex.

In 1941, President Franklin D. Roosevelt proclaimed the fifteenth of December as Bill of Rights Day. Only a week earlier, the United States had been attacked at Pearl Harbor and had been drawn into World War II. Because the enemies of the United States in that war were dictatorial governments, the President emphasized the differences between the opposing nations at war by contrasting the ideologies: the democratic aspirations contained in the Bill of Rights as opposed to the lack of individual freedom in the dictatorships. His speech on "The Four Freedoms," captured the imagination of the world.

Today and every day, Americans protect their freedom and liberty. They insist that state and national governments must not abridge the rights of citizens to the privileges of democracy, that all men and women be assured the benefits guaranteed by the Bill of Rights: life, liberty, and the pursuit of happiness.

ABOUT THE AUTHORS

ROBERT G. ALBION

Professor Albion, professor-emeritus of Oceanic History and Affairs at Harvard University, is now teaching at the University of Connecticut. He has contributed articles to encyclopedias, newspapers, and journals. Among his numerous books are *Introduction to Military History, The Rise of New York Port,* and *Seaports South of Sahara.*

RALPH K. ANDRIST

Mr. Andrist, a HERO Special Consultant, is a widely published author and award-winning radio news editor. He is author of *The Long Death: The Last Days of the Plain Indians.*

MARTIN BLUMENSON

Mr. Blumenson is a senior historian in the Office of the Chief of Military History, Department of the Army, and is a HERO Associate. He has written numerous articles for professional and scholarly publications and is the author of several books, including *Special Problems in the Korean Conflict; Anzio: The Battle that Failed;* and a forthcoming book, *The Reorganization of the Army, 1962.*

CLIFFORD S. DOWDEY

Mr. Dowdey is a lecturer in creative writing at the University of Richmond and is a HERO Special Consultant. He contributes articles to many journals, is known as a leading authority on the Civil War, is the author of *Lee's Last Campaign* and the editor and writer of *The Wartime Papers of R. E. Lee.*

R. ERNEST DUPUY, COLONEL, USA, RETIRED

Colonel R. E. Dupuy is a member of the Board of Directors and Chief Editor of HERO. In addition to over one hundred articles published in national encyclopedias, dictionaries, periodicals, and historical journals, he is the author of numerous books including *World in Arms, Men of West Point, Compact History of the United States Army,* and is co-author with his son of several books, including the *Compact History of the Civil War, Compact History of the Revolutionary War, Military Heritage of America,* and *Brave Men and Great Captains.*

TREVOR N. DUPUY, COLONEL, USA, RETIRED

Colonel T. N. Dupuy is the President and Executive Director of HERO and is a member of the Board of Directors. He has written numerous articles on historical, military, and national security subjects which have been published in encyclopedias and professional and scholarly journals. Among his many books are *Civil War Land Battles, Civil War Naval Actions,* a multivolume *Military History of World War II;* he is co-author with his father of several books (see above).

NORMAN A. GRAEBNER

Professor Graebner is a professor of history at the University of Illinois and is a HERO Associate. He is the author of articles and reviews in various journals; among his books are *Empire on the Pacific, The New Isolationism,* and *Cold War Diplomacy, 1945–1960.*

About the Authors

GAY M. HAMMERMAN

A research staff member on the Permanent Staff of HERO, Mrs. Hammerman was formerly a secondary school teacher of American history and government, has had editorial positions with the Departments of States and the Army, and has contributed to HERO historical studies.

EARL PARKER HANSON

Mr. Hanson is a Department of State Consultant to the Commonwealth of Puerto Rico and is a HERO Special Consultant. He is also a weekly columnist on world affairs for the San Juan *Island Times;* among his books are *Transformation, The Story of Modern Puerto Rico* and *Puerto Rico, Land of Wonders.*

GRACE P. HAYES

A research staff member on the Permanent Staff of HERO, Mrs. Hayes is the author of a classified two-volume history of the Pacific Theater in World War II and has contributed to HERO historical studies.

MARY F. HOYT

A research staff member on the Permanent Staff of HERO, Mrs. Hoyt was the coordinator for the *Holidays* book project and has contributed to other HERO historical studies. She has written numerous articles and is author of the forthcoming book, *Women in Space.*

RICHARD M. LEIGHTON

Dr. Leighton, a HERO Associate, is on the faculty of the Industrial College of the Armed Forces and is an assistant to the Senior Educational Advisor on curriculum matters. An author of numerous articles and reviews, Dr. Leighton has contributed to several books and is co-author of a forthcoming book, *Global Logistics and Strategy, 1943–1945.*

CHARLES B. MACDONALD

Mr. MacDonald, a HERO Associate, is Chief of the General History Branch in the Office of the Chief of Military History, Department of the Army. He contributes to professional and service journals and has written several books which include *The Siegfried Line Campaign* and *The Battle of the Huertgen Forest*.

WILLIAM MANGER

Professor Manger, a HERO Associate, is Director of the Latin American Studies Program at Georgetown University. He is a lecturer on Inter-American Regional Organization and Relations and Latin American Government and Politics, and has written numerous articles and papers on these subjects. He is author of *Basic Principles of the Inter-American System* and *Pan American Postwar Organization*.

ROLLIE E. POPPINO

Dr. Poppino is an assistant professor of history at the University of California at Davis and serves as a Special Consultant to HERO. His articles and reviews have appeared in numerous publications and he has authored a forthcoming book, *International Communism in Latin America, 1917–1963*.

ARMIN RAPPAPORT

Professor Rappaport, Department of History of the University of California at Berkeley, is a HERO Associate. He is the author of *The Navy League of the United States* and *Henry L. Stimson and Japan, 1931–1933* in addition to being the editor of *The War with Mexico, The Monroe Doctrine,* and *Issues in American Diplomacy*.

About the Authors

GUNTHER E. ROTHENBERG

Professor Rothenberg, a HERO Associate, is an associate professor in the Department of History at the University of New Mexico. He is the author of *The Austrian Military Border in Croatia: 1522–1747* and *The Austrian Border Regiments in Croatia: 1740–1882*.

WALTER RUNDELL, JR.

Dr. Rundell, Assistant Executive Secretary of the American Historical Association, is a HERO Special Consultant; he is the author of *Concepts of the Frontier and the West* and contributes to scholarly and professional journals.

MAX SAVELLE

Professor Savelle is a professor of American history at the University of Washington and is a HERO Special Consultant. He is the author of *The United States Colonial Period* and *Colonial Origin of American Thought*.

JOHN A. SCHUTZ

Professor Schutz is in the Department of History and Social Science at Whittier College and is a HERO Special Consultant. Among his books are *Thomas Pownall: British Defender of American Liberty* and *William Shirley;* he has also written numerous reviews and articles for professional and scholarly journals.

BOYD C. SHAFER

Mr. Shafer, recently Executive Secretary of the American Historical Association, has been editor of the *American Historical Review* since 1953. A Special Consultant to HERO, Mr. Shafer has written many articles on history and social science; among his books are *Life, Liberty, and the Pursuit of Bread,* and *Nationalism, Myth, and Reality*.

CHARLES H. WESLEY

Dr. Wesley is the President of Central State College and is a HERO Special Consultant. He has written *Richard Allen: Apostle of Freedom* and *Collapse of the Confederacy*.

RELATED BOOKS OF INTEREST

NATIONAL FREEDOM DAY

Douglass, Frederick. *The Life and Times of Frederick Douglass, Written By Himself.* Hartford: Park Publishing Co., 1884.

Dumond, Dwight L. *The Emancipation Proclamation: Freedom in the Fullness of Time.* Ann Arbor: University of Michigan Press, 1963.

Durman, Donald C. *He Belongs to the Ages: The Statues of Abraham Lincoln.* Ann Arbor: University of Michigan Press, 1951.

Franklin, John Hope. *The Emancipation Proclamation.* New York: Doubleday & Company, Inc., 1963.

Freedom to the Free—1863–1963. Century of Emancipation. A Report to the President by the United States Commission on Civil Rights, 1963. Washington, D.C.: U.S. Government Printing Office, 1963.

Logan, Rayford W. *The Negro in American Life and Thought: The Nadir, 1877–1901.* New York: The Dial Press, Inc., 1954.

McLaughlin, Andrew C. *A Constitutional History of the United States.* New York: Appleton-Century-Crofts, 1935.

Quarles, Benjamin. *Abraham Lincoln and the Negro.* New York: Oxford University Press, Inc., 1962.

Randall, James G., and Donald, David. *The Divided Union.* Boston: Little, Brown & Co., 1961.

Washington, Booker T. *Up From Slavery: An Autobiography.* New York: Doubleday & Company, Inc., 1926.

Wesley, Charles H. *The Thirteenth Amendment. A Milestone in Emancipation.* Washington, D.C.: The Graduate School, Howard University Press, 1940.

————. *Ohio Negroes in the Civil War.* Civil War Centennial Commission. Columbus: Ohio State University Press, 1962.

Who's Who in Colored America, 1933–1937. A Biographical Dictionary of Notable Living Persons of African Descent in America. 4th ed. Brooklyn: Who's Who in Colored America, 1937.

Wilson, Henry. *History of the Rise and Fall of the Slave Power in America.* Vol. III. Boston: Osgood & Co., 1877.

Wilson, Joseph T. *Emancipation, Its Courses and Progress.* Hampton, Va.: Normal School Steam Power Press Print, 1882.

Wilson, Prince E. "Celebration of 'June Teenth' by Negro Texans." A memo. Wilberforce, Ohio: Central State College, 1964.

Woodson, Carter G., and Wesley, Charles H. *The Story of the Negro Retold.* Washington, D.C.: Associated Publishers, 1959.

————. *The Negro in Our History.* Washington, D.C.: Associated Publishers, Inc., 1962.

GEORGE WASHINGTON'S BIRTHDAY

Cunliffe, Marcus. *George Washington: Man and Monument.* Boston: Little, Brown and Company, 1958.

Dupuy, R. Ernest and Trevor N. *The Compact History of the Revolutionary War.* New York: Hawthorn Books, Inc., 1963.

Freeman, Douglas Southall. *George Washington: A Biography.* 7 vols. New York: Charles Scribner's Sons, 1947–1958.

McKown, Robin. *Washington's America.* New York: Grosset & Dunlap, Inc., 1961.

Mayo, Bernard. *Myths and Men: Patrick Henry, George Washington, Thomas Jefferson.* Athens, Georgia: University of Georgia Press, 1959.

ALAMO DAY

Binkley, William C. *The Texas Revolution.* Baton Rouge: Louisiana State University Press, 1952.

Calcott, Wilfrid Hardy. *Santa Anna, the Story of an Enigma Who Once Was Mexico.* Norman: University of Oklahoma Press, 1936. Hamden, Connecticut: Archon Books, 1964. Reprint.

Friend, Llerena. *Sam Houston, the Great Designer.* Austin: University of Texas Press, 1954.

James, Marquis. *The Raven.* Indianapolis: Bobbs-Merrill, 1929. New York: Paperback Library (54–144). Paperback reprint.

Lord, Walter. *A Time to Stand: The Story of the Alamo*. New York: Harper, 1961. New York: Affiliated Publishers, Inc. (Pocket Book 7023). Paperback reprint.

Richardson, Rupert N. *Texas, the Lone Star State*. Englewood Cliffs, New Jersey: Prentice-Hall, Inc., 1958.

Tinkle, Lon. *Thirteen Days to Glory: the Siege of the Alamo*. New York: McGraw-Hill, 1958. New York: New American Library (Signet S1776). Paperback reprint.

LOYALTY DAY

Barth, Alan. *The Loyalty of Free Men*. Hamden, Conn.: Shoe String Press, Inc., 1951.

Commager, Henry Steele. *The American Mind*. New Haven, Conn.: Yale University Press, 1950. Paperback reprint, 1959.

Curti, Merle. *The Growth of American Thought*. 3rd ed. New York: Harper & Row, 1964.

———. *The Roots of American Loyalty*. New York: Brown Book Co., 1946.

Dahl, Robert A. *A Preface to Democratic Theory*. Chicago: The University of Chicago Press, 1956. Paperback reprint, 1963.

Gabriel, Ralph H. *The Course of American Democratic Thought*. 2nd ed. New York: The Ronald Press Co., 1956.

Padover, Saul K. *The Meaning of Democracy: An Appraisal of the American Experience*. New York: Frederick A. Praeger, Publisher, 1963, and paperback edition.

Persons, Stow. *American Minds: A History of Ideas.* New York: Holt, Rinehart & Winston, Inc., 1958.

Wecter, Dixon. *The Hero in America.* Ann Arbor: University of Michigan Press, 1963, and paperback edition.

The best single volume is Curti's *The Roots of American Loyalty.*

CINCO DE MAYO

Bancroft, Hubert Howe. *Popular History of the Mexican People.* San Francisco: History Company, 1887.

Dabbs, Jack Autrey. *The French Army in Mexico 1861–1867: A Study in Military Government.* The Hague: Mouton & Co., 1963.

Díaz, Porfirio. *Archivo del General Porfirio Díaz.* Tomo I (vol. 1). Mexico, D. F.: Editorial "Elde," 1947.

García Loya, Diego. *Mosaic of Mexican History.* Mexico, D. F.: Editorial Cultura, 1958.

Parkes, Henry Bamford. *A History of Mexico.* 3rd ed. Boston: Houghton Mifflin Company, 1960.

Roeder, Ralph. *Juárez and His Mexico.* Vol. II. New York: Viking Press, 1947.

Simpson, Lesley Byrd. *Many Mexicos.* 3rd ed. Berkeley and Los Angeles: University of California Press, 1960. Paperback.

ARMED FORCES DAY

Dupuy, R. Ernest, and Dupuy, Trevor N. *Military Heritage of America.* New York: McGraw-Hill, Inc., 1956.

Dupuy, R. Ernest. *Compact History of the U.S. Army.* Rev. 2nd ed. New York: Hawthorn Books, Inc., 1961.

——. *Men of West Point.* New York: William Sloane Associates, 1951.

——. *Where They Have Trod.* Philadelphia. J. B. Lippincott Co., 1940.

Glines, Carroll V., Jr. *Compact History of the U.S. Air Force.* New York: Hawthorn Books, Inc., 1963.

Pierce, Philip N., and Hough, Frank O. *Compact History of the U.S. Marine Corps.* Rev. 2nd ed. New York: Hawthorn Books, Inc., 1964.

Pratt, Fletcher. *Compact History of the U.S. Navy.* Rev. 2nd ed. New York: Hawthorn Books, Inc., 1962.

FLAG DAY

Hazeltine, Mary E. *Anniversaries and Holidays.* Chicago: American Library Association, 1944.

Kannik, Preben. *The Flag Book.* New York: M. Barrows and Company, 1957.

Krythe, Maymie R. *All about American Holidays.* New York: Harper & Row, 1962.

Quaife, Milo M. *et al. The History of the United States Flag.* New York: Harper & Row, 1961. Published in cooperation with the Eastern National Park and Monument Association.

Schauffler, Robert H., editor. *Plays for Our American Holidays.* New York: Dodd, Mead & Company, 1928.

Related Books of Interest

V-J DAY

END OF JAPANESE WAR

Butow, R. J. C. *Japan's Decision to Surrender*. Stanford, Calif.: Stanford University Press, 1954.

Feis, Herbert. *Japan Subdued: The Atomic Bomb and the End of the War in the Pacific*. Princeton, N.J.: Princeton University Press, 1961.

BEGINNING OF JAPANESE WAR

Cole, Wayne S. "American Entry into World War II: A Historiographical Appraisal," *Mississippi Valley Historical Review*. XLIII (1957), pp. 595–617.

Drummond, D. F. *The Passing of American Neutrality*. Ann Arbor: University of Michigan Press, 1955.

Feis, Herbert. *The Road to Pearl Harbor*. Princeton, N.J.: Princeton University Press, 1950.

CITIZENSHIP DAY

Adamic, Louis. *Nation of Nations*. New York: Harper & Row, 1945.

Handlin, Oscar. *Immigration as a Factor in American History*. Englewood Cliffs, New Jersey: Prentice-Hall, Inc., 1959. Paperback.

———. *The Uprooted*. Boston: Little, Brown and Company, 1951. New York: Grosset & Dunlap, Inc., 1957. Paperback reprint.

Kennedy, John F. *A Nation of Immigrants*. Revised and enlarged. New York: Harper & Row, 1964.

Van Doren, Carl. *The Great Rehearsal*. New York: Viking Press, 1948. New York: Viking Press (Compass C23), 1961. Paperback reprint.

Welch, Joseph N. *The Constitution*. Boston: Houghton Mifflin Company, 1956.

AMERICAN INDIAN DAY

American Heritage Book of Indians. New York: American Heritage, 1961.

Fey, H. E., and McNickle, D'Arcy. *Indians and Other Americans*. New York: Harper & Row, 1959.

Hagan, William T. *American Indians*. Chicago: The University of Chicago Press, 1961. Paperback. (Scholarly but brief and readable.)

Josephy, Alvin M., Jr. *Patriot Chiefs*. New York: The Viking Press, Inc., 1961. (Stories of the lives and careers of some of the famous Indian leaders: King Philip, Tecumseh, Crazy Horse, Chief Joseph, etc.)

Wissler, Clark. *Indians of the United States*. New York: Doubleday & Company, Inc., 1939.

LEIF ERICSON DAY

Donovan, Frank R., editor. "The Vikings," *Horizon Magazine*. New York: Harper and Row, 1964.

Hermann, Paul. *Conquest by Man.* Translated by Michael Bullock. New York: Harper & Bros., 1954.

Holand, Hjalmar R. *Explorations in America Before Columbus.* New York: Twayne Publishers, Inc., 1956.

Hovgaard, William. *The Voyages of the Norsemen to America.* New York: The American-Scandinavian Foundation, 1914.

Ingstad, Helge. "Vinland Ruins Prove Vikings Found the New World," *National Geographic Magazine.* Washington: November 1964.

Pohl, Frederick J. *The Lost Discovery: Uncovering the Track of the Vikings in America.* New York: W. W. Norton & Co., Inc., out of print.

Shippen, Katherine B. *Leif Eriksson: First Voyager to America.* New York: Harper & Bros., 1951.

Thordason, Matthias. *The Vinland Voyages.* New York: American Geographical Society, Research Series No. 18, 1930.

THANKSGIVING DAY

Chicago Public Library. *Hallowe'en, Thanksgiving Day, Christmas, New Year's Day.* A bibliography.

Earle, Alice M. *Customs and Fashion in Old New England.* New York: Charles Scribner's Sons, 1899.

Linton, Ralph. *We Gather Together; The Story of Thanksgiving.* New York: Abelard-Schuman Limited, 1949.

Lore, William de L. *The Fast and Thanksgiving Day of New England.* Boston: Houghton Mifflin Company, 1895.

INDEX

Index

Index

394.26

Holidays. U. S.

JAN 24 1966
T 1/372
MAY 20
15

JAN 12
MAY 30